KU-203-303

REGENT'S
UNIVERSITY LONDON
WITHDRAWN

The Language of Meetings

Malcolm Goodale

English Language Teacher
at the United Nations in Geneva

With illustrations by Mike Gordon

FOR
REFERENCE ONLY

TELEPEN

703988 03

THOMSON

HEINLE

Australia Canada Mexico Singapore Spain United Kingdom United States

THOMSON
™
HEINLE

The Language of Meetings
Malcolm Goodale

Publisher/Global ELT: *Christopher Wenger*
Executive Marketing Manager/Global ELT/ESL: *Amy Mabley*

REGENT'S COLLEGE
ACC. No. 70398803
CLASS 808.5 GOO
S.I.
KEY

Copyright © 1987 Heinle, a division of Thomson Learning, Inc.
Thomson Learning™ is a trademark used herein under license.
Previously published by LTP.

Printed in the UK

12 13 14 15   06 05 04 03 02

For more information contact Heinle, 25 Thomson Place, Boston, MA 02210 USA,
or you can visit our Internet site at http://www.heinle.com

All rights reserved. No part of this work covered by the copyright hereon may be reproduced or
used in any form or by any means—graphic, electronic, or mechanical, including photocopying,
recording, taping, Web distribution or information storage and retrieval systems—without the
written permission of the publisher.

For permission to use material from this text or product contact us:
Tel   1-800-730-2214
Fax   1-800-730-2215
Web   www.thomsonrights.com

ISBN: 0-906717-46-9

Author's Note
This one is for my Mum and Dad and the baby. I'd also like to thank Kâmuran, Murat and Kaplan
for their love and support. I mustn't forget to thank my students for the help they've given me during
the writing of this book.

Many thanks to Michael Lewis for his guidance and contributions.

The author is a teacher at The United Nations in Geneva. The views expressed herein do not
necessarily reflect the views of The United Nations.

Acknowledgements
We are grateful to the following for permission to use copyright material Punch Publications, for
several cartoons. IPM Personnel Management Services Ltd for an extract from *Negotiating in
Practice* by K. Sissons; Collins and Edward De Bono for an extract from *Tactics, the Art and
Science of Success*. Century Hutchinson and the authors for short extracts from *Getting to Yes*.

CONTENTS

How to get the best from this book

Many professionals—diplomats, agency representatives, and business people—have to take part in meetings which are conducted in English. The language of such meetings follows definite patterns. Even if your English is good, not all of the language of meetings is obvious.

This book presents and teaches all the language you need to participate effectively in meetings in English.

The language is divided into 12 units. Most of these follow a similar format, and can be studied in any order. The first and last units are slightly different:

Unit 1 General Language Points

You are advised to study this unit first. It identifies, explains, and practises 10 key areas of language use which are particularly important in the language used in meetings.

This unit is very like the sort of material you find in a good general language teaching textbook. There are explanations and practices to focus your attention on the important language.

Unit 12 Procedure for Formal Meetings

There are many kinds of meeting, and different degrees of formality. The most formal is a meeting directed from the chair. The language used in these meetings, particularly by the person in the chair, is very stylised. If you have to run a meeting in English, you simply need a list of the phrases which are used in the different situations which arise during such a meeting. There is a certain amount of special vocabulary, and a long list of standard phrases. These are presented, with notes, in Unit 12.

This will only be of interest for people who need to run meetings in English. It can be studied at any time, and is placed last only for convenience.

Units 2-11

Each of these units concentrates on a specific language area. You can study the units in any order, so that, for example, if you find it difficult to interrupt during meetings, you can look immediately at Unit 5. In general the language in the units does not get more difficult as you go through the book. On the other hand, *what you are doing* with the language does get more difficult. It is more difficult to work out a compromise, which involves negotiating to and fro with another person than it is to present your own argument, or interrupt. You are advised to study the units in the order in which they occur, so that you will slowly be building from simpler situations to more complicated discussions and negotiations.

Each of these units follows a similar pattern. It will help you to get the best out of your studies if you understand how each section is designed.

Language awareness

Before studying a certain area, you are invited to think of the language you would use during a meeting to achieve certain objectives *relying on the language you already know*. We suggest you do not write these phrases into the book, but make a note of them on a piece of paper.

You can do this alone, or, better, with one or two fellow students. It does not matter whether you find "right answers" at this stage. The idea is to focus your attention on the language you need for a particular part of the meeting.

The Language and notes

The next two pages of each unit represent the core of this book. You will find a comprehensive inventory of the language needed for a particular area.

In general, the first two or three phrases under each heading are the most useful or the most general. You have to choose whether to learn some, or all, of the phrases. Think about the kind of meetings you attend, and the situations where you will need to use English in meetings. Do not just learn indiscriminately — select, and then try to learn your chosen phrases *exactly*. Sometimes, changing one or two words can change the meaning, or the strength, of the phrase considerably.

There are notes to help you. These will help you to understand the phrases and deal with difficult points of grammar. In the notes, you are sometimes presented with alternatives. These are always presented like this:

I have ¹certain ²reservations about . . .   1. ▷ serious — stronger
                                                  2. ▷ misgivings

If the note contains this symbol ▷, the word which follows can be substituted directly into the phrase; if it does not have that symbol it provides you with a comment, or explanation which **cannot** be directly substituted.

Check yourself

The next page of each unit contains a selected list of the most useful phrases presented on the previous two pages. Here, words are missed out, and each missing word is replaced by a line.

When you think you have learned the phrases, you can look at this page and check to make sure that you can remember the *exact* words of the phrases you have learned. You can also use this page as an *aide-memoire* while you are doing the first of the mini-meetings which follow.

Mini-meetings

Each unit contains at least two mini-meetings. In these, the structure of part of a discussion, negotiation or argument is presented. It needs the language presented earlier in the unit. You are asked to practise these using either any topic you like, perhaps drawn from your own business or interest, or one of the topics suggested in the unit.

There is a very important point here. The language of meetings is full of standard phrases. These phrases are the same whether they are used to discuss nuclear warfare, arrangements for booking the hall for the amateur dramatic society's annual show, marketing difficulties with a new product, or a Housing Association discussion on replanting the gardens.

Some professionals who need English in meetings, prefer to practise the language of meetings by talking about the topics they will need in their work. If you, and your fellow students, would like to do this, you can do it with the language presented in this book. Other professionals, however, like to use their English classes as an opportunity to forget the content of work for a while. If you'd like to do this, you can still practise the language of meetings perfectly seriously, by discussing the general, social, and even light-hearted, topics proposed for the mini-meetings.

Experience has shown that it is often easier to remember the language of meetings if you practise in a light-hearted relaxed way, and concentrate on the language of meetings, rather than the content of what you say. Don't make the mini-meetings too serious, otherwise they will inhibit, rather than develop your learning.

Match and Complete

Each unit contains five of these practices. These can be done at any time during the unit, but help to focus your attention on some of the most important collocations (groups of words which often occur together) which are used in meetings. If you wish to speak fluently and effectively in meetings, it is not a matter of learning more vocabulary or more grammar, but of learning more phrases (mentioned above) and *groups* of words. These practices help to do this. If you study this section carefully, you will master about 100 important prepositional phrases, and about 150 important collocations.

Each of these expressions is presented followed by a sentence which should provide you with enough context that you do not need to spend a lot of time with your dictionary.

Discussion

Each unit ends with a piece of authentic material — material written for professionals who use English in meetings. Some discuss how people negotiate. Some are light-hearted, and discuss things that can go wrong in meetings.

These discussions are to help you get to know your fellow students better, and to give you the opportunity to think about and talk about what happens in meetings.

To make you even more aware of meetings, your behaviour in meetings, and the language of meetings, the book is illustrated with cartoons and quotations. These are partly to amuse, partly to help your memory, and partly to make you think more clearly about meetings. One of the most important quotations is this

> *Nine out of ten businessmen believe half the time they spend in meetings to be wasted.*

We hope that **The Language of Meetings** will help you to be more confident in using your English in meetings, and will lead you to the conclusion that more of the time **you** spend in meetings is effective and useful.

Those who are unable to learn from past meetings are condemned to repeat them.

1 Language of Meetings

General Language Points

We always say exactly what we mean:

a. in life.

b. in meetings .

Do you agree? Can you give some examples?

Discuss

Work in pairs or small groups. How have the speakers changed the way they express themselves so that their message is more effective?

This language may seem ridiculous when you read it, but in a diplomatic or business discussion this language is perfectly normal, and only takes a few seconds to say.

Can you give examples from your own language of how a basic message is presented in different language to make it more socially acceptable or effective?

Effective communication in meetings is partly a matter of knowing certain special expressions. Many of these are given in this book. Some of the ways we change the basic message are, however, generalisable. Look again at the example above; how many of these features did you notice?

1. Using *would, could* or *might* to make what you say more tentative.

2. Presenting your view as a question not a statement.

3. Using a grammatical negative (adding *n't*) to make a suggestion more open and therefore more negotiable.

4. Using an introductory phrase to prepare the listener for your message.

5. Adding I'*m afraid* to make clear that you recognise the unhelpfulness of your response.

6. Using words which qualify or restrict what you say to make your position more flexible (*a bit* difficult, *a slight* problem).

7. Using *not* with a positive word instead of the obvious negative word (*not very convenient, I don't agree*).

8. Using a comparative (*better, more convenient*) to soften your message.

9. Using a continuous form (I *was wondering*) instead of a simple form (I *wondered*) to make a suggestion more flexible.

10. Using stress as an important way of making the message more effective (It **is** important . . .)

All of these features are common in the language in this book. Before studying the specific language needed for effective communication in meetings, here is an opportunity to practise the most general features of English which occur again and again in the book.

1. Using *would.*

Would is often added to make any statement more tentative. It takes away the dogmatic tone of many statements.

That is unacceptable.	**That would be unacceptable.**
That does not meet our requirements.	**That would not meet our requirements.**
We need further reassurance.	**We would need further reassurance.**

Put *would* in the following:

1. That is too late.

2. I prefer to meet before that.

3. We expect them to accept our proposals.

4. We hope to be able to complete before the end of the year.

5. Flying has definite advantages.

6. I'm not able to give a guarantee at this stage.

7. Finance is no problem.

8. I don't agree.

9. I'm afraid I don't accept that.

2. Questions

Often suggestions are presented in question form:

That is too late.   →   **Is that too late?**
That would be too late.   →   **Would that be too late?**

Change these suggestions into questions.

1. Flying would have advantages.
2. Friday would be convenient.
3. We would need another meeting fairly soon.
4. We could ask the UN to finance the project.
5. It would be a good idea to involve the French.
6. We could cancel.
7. We've got to increase our offer.
8. They can raise some of the finance themselves.

3. Adding *n't* to suggestions.

The examples above all sound more tentative and negotiable if they are grammatically negative:

Isn't that too late?
Wouldn't that be too late?

Change the other examples in the same way.

4. Introductory phrases.

Often we introduce our reaction with a word or phrase which tells the listener what kind of comment we are going to make. In particular some phrases warn the listener that disagreement follows. Here are the most common introductory phrases. Which ones are warnings?

Actually,	**With respect,**	**In those circumstances,**
Well,	**To be honest,**	**In fact,**
Frankly,	**As a matter of fact,**	**To put it bluntly,**

"Actually, George, the financial picture isn't too bright here at Head Office."

5. I'm afraid.

The most common phrase in spoken English to show that the speaker recognises that his/her reaction is in some way unhelpful or unwelcome is I'm afraid. It may warn of disagreement, but its general meaning is wider and indicates the speaker sees his/her reaction as *unavoidably unhelpful*:

Could I speak to Jack please?
I'm afraid he's out of the country at the moment.

Would next Tuesday be convenient?
I'm afraid I'm tied up all day.

Reply to these naturally but using I'm *afraid*.
1. Can we meet again later this week?
2. Couldn't we ask the IMF to fund us?
3. Wouldn't it be a good idea to involve the Americans?
4. Could you guarantee delivery by late September?
5. Do you know the Chairman personally?
6. Have you got last year's figures yet?
7. Where's the report?
8. I thought you were going to bring the details today?

6. Qualifiers.

Successful meetings often depend on avoiding direct disagreement. The more general the statement, the more likely it is to produce disagreement. Not surprisingly, therefore, good negotiators often restrict general statements by using qualifiers. Here are some of the most common qualifiers in English:

a **slight** misunderstanding   a **short** delay

a **little bit too** early   a **bit of a** problem

some reservations   a **little** more time

Add qualifiers to these:
1. That would leave me with a problem.
2. I have doubts about that.
3. We need more time.
4. We have production difficulties.
5. We have had a disagreement with our German colleagues.
6. We need changes before I can give the proposal my unqualified support.

Now say these things in an acceptable way using similar language:
7. I don't want to meet as early as that.
8. If you do that you'll leave me in a mess with my Personnel Manager.
9. I can't accept such a tight schedule.
10. How could you possibly think that's what I meant!

7. *Not* + *very* + positive adjective.

Often English avoids negative adjectives, preferring *not* + positive equivalent:

The hotel was dirty.	→	**The hotel wasn't very clean.**
The food was cold.	→	**The food was not very hot.**

Change these in a similar way:

1. That's inconvenient.
2. That's unsuitable.
3. That's a stupid suggestion.
4. This year's figures are bad.
5. That's a negative way of looking at the problem.
6. That proposal is insensitive to local conditions.
7. That suggestion is impractical.
8. That was an unhelpful remark.
9. That's a destructive approach.
10. That's a useless line of argument.
11. I'm unhappy with that idea.

This feature is not only true with an adjective construction. Notice these examples:

I disagree completely.	**I don't agree at all.**
I dislike that idea.	**I don't like that idea at all.**
I reject what you say.	**I don't accept what you say.**

"There's a bit of a discussion going on out there in the middle . . ."

8. Comparatives

In offering an alternative suggestion, the comparative is often used:

Wouldn't the 31st be more convenient? It might be cheaper to go by air .

The implication is that the other person's suggestion is acceptable, but yours is **more** acceptable. For this reason the use of the comparative is more tactful.

Offer these proposals, using a comparative, and an appropriate verb form including, for example, *would, might,* etc.

1. It's appropriate to wait a a few weeks.
2. An earlier delivery date is helpful.
3. It's a good idea to take a long term view.
4. It's dangerous to delay a decision.
5. Mr. Carlos is a good person to approach.
6. The World Bank is anxious to support this kind of project.

Sometimes comparative phrases, not including adjectives, are used. You will need them in these examples:

7. NGOs provide funds for projects like this.
8. The Belgian plant has capacity in the short term.
9. Research is needed before we make a decision.

9. Continuous forms

In English, the simple past is used if the speaker sees the event as a single whole, while the past continuous is used if the speaker sees the event "stretched out" in time. For this reason the continuous form of the verb is more flexible, because the event can be "interrupted", while the simple past is more often used to express facts or events seen as finished and complete.
Look at these pairs. Can you see any differences between them? Discuss them in small groups, and then compare your ideas with the whole group and with your teacher.

1. I tried to ring you yesterday.
   I was trying to ring you yesterday.

2. We intended to make new arrangements for next year.
   We were intending to make new arrangements for next year.

3. I wondered if you'd come to a decision yet.
   I was wondering if you'd come to a decision yet.

4. We hoped you'd accept 8%.
   We were hoping you'd accept 8%.

5. We discussed the problem yesterday.
   We were discussing the problem yesterday.

Notice, in every case the simple past gives the impression that the speaker means "this is what I/we did before we started our present discussion"; it gives the impression that the person s/he is speaking to is **excluded.**
In contrast, the continuous form, used with verbs like *hope, discuss* etc., gives the impression of **including** the other partner in the discussion. For this reason continuous forms seem more friendly and open, and are often appropriate if you are trying to engage the other person in an open negotiation.

10. Stressed words

Grammar and vocabulary are, of course, important in getting your meaning across. Less obviously, but equally importantly, the words which you give special stress to can change the meaning of what you say. Contrast this pair;

It's rather a **large** house.
It's **rather** a large house.

The most important use of this kind is the word *quite*. If *quite* is stressed, it is a **qualification** (**quite** interested, but not very), but if the following adjective is stressed, quite means **very** (quite **interested**).

Say these examples so that you give the meaning **very:**

1. We're quite interested in your suggestion.
2. We were quite pleased with their proposal.
3. We will be quite disappointed if we can't reach agreement today.
4. We think that's quite a useful contribution to the discussion.
5. He's quite capable of helping us out of our difficulties.
6. The new figures are quite exciting.

Stress **quite** in these examples — make sure you understand how strong or weak each phrase is:

7. That's quite different from our own suggestion.
8. We're quite satisfied with the preliminary figures.
9. We're quite certain we can deliver by the end of the month.

Remember, native speakers often use *quite* instead of *very*, but if it has the meaning of *very*, it is the word following *quite* which receives the heavy stress.

Stressed auxiliaries

Many English verb forms which look the same on paper, have two different forms in speech. In one case, the auxiliary verb, or part of the verb **(be)** is stressed, and in the other case this word is unstressed. The two sentences do not mean the same thing. Usually parts of **(be)** in auxiliary verbs in English are unstressed. Sometimes, there is a special way of writing these unstressed forms:

I'**ve** sent you the details already.
It'**s** four o'clock.

Sometimes, there is no special way of writing them but they are unstressed, and weakly pronounced:

We can make alternative arrangements. /kən/ not /kan/
We could meet again tomorrow. /kəd/ not /kud/

In every case, however, it is possible to give a heavy stress to the normally unstressed part of **(be)** or the auxiliary. If you do this, it shows special emotion is attached to what you say. It can be used to correct the other person:

I thought you were Belgian.
I **am** Belgian.

Or to give special emotion to what you say. Different emotions are possible — annoyance or surprise, for example. It is very difficult to use these patterns effectively, and you may be wiser to avoid them yourself. If you are listening to native speakers, however, it is important that you recognise the emotional force behind what they are saying.

Discuss what you think the speaker means if s/he says the following:

1. We **have** sent you the details already.
2. We **could** meet again tomorrow.
3. It **is** five o'clock.
4. We **are** waiting for your decision.
5. We **are** expecting a prompt reply.
6. We **have** tried to keep you fully informed.
7. We **were** disappointed.
8. We **do** need at least four months notice.
9. We **did** expect to make a decision today.
10. This question **does** need to be resolved very soon.

The language points discussed in this unit are general features of English. The features in English may be very different from your own language. It is up to you to decide if you want to use all of the language points discussed here. It is essential, however, if you are going to use English in meetings with native speakers, you are aware of the way they use English to make their message more direct, more tactful, more diplomatic etc.

Collocations

As well as vocabulary, grammar, and stress, there is another important way in which you can improve your control of the language of meetings. Certain words often occur together — *a short term solution, a high priority*. There are a very large number of these collocations (groups of words which often occur together) which are used in the language of meetings. We have identified more than 150 of these for you. They are spread through the different units of this book. Each of the exercises is similar, and arranged like the one below. Here is what you should do:

1. Alone, or in pairs or small groups, look at the words at the top of each **Match and Complete** activity. Try, without writing anything down, to make collocations using a word from the column on the left with one from the column on the right. In every case there is only one way that you can make all five collocations correctly in the activities. If you are left with words which you do not think make a correct pair, you will need to think again about the pairs you have already made.

2. When you have made five successful phrases, report them to the whole group, and agree on the correct phrases.

3. We suggest that, even now, you do not write them in your book. Instead, we suggest you try to fit each collocation into one of the example sentences which follow. Again, you can only do this in one way so that all the collocations fit.

4. We suggest that a few days or a week later you look again at the collocations, and write in the ones you can remember which you are sure are correct. You can use the sentences again to check. (The answers are given on page 127/128.)

When you are sure that you can identify the collocations correctly, you can write them in so that, as you work your way through the book, you will make for yourself a complete list of the correct collocations. Remember, writing the correct collocations into your book will help you to remember them — but don't do this when you meet them for the first time.

Match and Complete

a vested	step	_____
a foregone	point	_____
a disastrous	interest	_____
a stop-gap	conclusion	_____
a debatable	solution	_____

1. It was a _____: everybody knew he'd get the job.

2. That's a _____. One should consider both sides of the problem and I can see merit in both of them.

3. As a _____ I'm in favour, but we mustn't forget that we still need to find something more permanent.

4. We have a _____ in John's election, because if Henry is elected, we'll never get promoted.

5. Leaving the organization would be a _____ as far as his career is concerned.

Group Work

Work in small groups. Look at the following "basic dialogues". Using some of the language features discussed in this unit try to write the dialogue in language which is more suitable for the language of meetings .

1. My price is fair.
   I agree.

2. A bridge is better than a tunnel.
   I prefer the tunnel.

3. That is acceptable if you promise to deliver by the end of August.
   Impossible! But we promise the end of September.

4. We hope you'll allow us 10% margin.
   We can't. We expected you to suggest 5%.

5. What's the maximum you'll offer?
   What's the minimum you'll accept?
   Be more helpful!
   Be more helpful yourself!

   ....

Discussion

Working in English — Advantages and Disadvantages

Work in groups of 3 or 4 and decide whether you agree with the following statements. If you do, decide if it is an advantage or disadvantage for you.

1. Foreigners can ask for a repetition more than any native speaker could.
2. You are shown more respect because you are working in a foreign language.
3. Native speakers have more patience with foreigners.
4. Non-native speakers can always change their minds later by saying that they misunderstood.
5. You may not understand everything that is said to you.
6. You may have problems expressing what you want to say.
7. Native speakers notice, and are affected by, all your grammatical mistakes.
8. You may not understand all the non-verbal behaviour of native speakers.
9. Some of your non-verbal behaviour will not be understood by native speakers.
10. You understand English (or American) culture more than the English (or Americans) understand your culture.

What do you think are the main effects, advantages and disadvantages, of international groups using English when they meet together?

2 Presenting an Argument

Language Awareness

How do you:

1. Begin to present what you want to say?

2. Change to a new point?

3. Add another point to your argument?

4. Give an example?

5. Contrast one point with another?

6. Make a generalisation?

7. Say you prefer one thing to another?

8. Finish what you want to say?

Beginning

I [1]would like to begin by . . .

I would like to make a few remarks concerning . . .

I would like to comment on the problem of . . .

I would like to [2]mention [3]briefly that . . .

There are [4]three points I'd like to make.

The most important points seem to me to be . . .

1. ▷ wish — most formal.
   ▷ should like — more formal
   ▷ want — informal.
2. Suggests you are not going to speak for a long time.
   ▷ touch upon.
3. Suggests that you are not going to speak for long.
4. ▷ two.
   ▷ several.
   ▷ a number of.

Ordering

First of all, we must [1]bear in mind . . .

At the [2]outset . . .

To begin with . . .

[3]Firstly, . . . Secondly, . . . Thirdly, ... Finally, . . .

Simple, but important, as they help the listener to understand your view.
1. Consider. Often used in the passive: *There are three points which should be borne in mind.*
2. Beginning.
3. Do not confuse with *at first* which contrasts with *later*: *At first I hated English, but now I love it.*
   ▷ First, second, etc — more formal.

Introducing a New Point

I would now like to turn briefly to the problem of . . .

The next [1]issue I would like to [2]focus on is . . .

Turning to . . .

1. Question.
   ▷ concentrate.

Adding

In addition, . . .

I [1]might add that . . .

As well as . . ., there is also . . .

Not only . . ., but also . . .

Furthermore, . . .

Moreover, . . .

1. ▷ could — less definitive.

Giving an Example

[1]Let me give an example . . .

To illustrate this point, let us consider . . .

[2]A case in point is . . .

1. *Let* is followed by an infinitive without *to*.
2. An example.

Balancing

On the one hand . . ., but on the other hand . . .

Although . . ., we mustn't forget . . .

[1]Whereas . . ., we have to remember . . .

[2]In spite of . . ., I still think . . .

[2]Despite the fact that . . ., I . . .

1. Expresses contrast.
2. *in spite of* and *despite* are interchangeable; *despite* is more formal.

Generalising

On the whole, . . .

In general, . . .

[1]Generally speaking, . . .

By and large, . . .

All in all, . . .

All things considered, . . .

1. ▷ broadly.

Stating Preferences

I'd rather . . . than . . .

I prefer . . . to . . .

I tend to favour . . . as opposed to . . .

. . . has an advantage over . . . in that . . .

The main advantage of . . . is that . . .

Concluding

Let me conclude by saying . . .

I'd like to conclude by stating that . . .

Allow me to conclude by [1]highlighting the fact that . . .

In conclusion, I would like to [2]reiterate that . . .

I would now like to conclude my comments by reassuring you that we are fully aware of the fact that . . .

1. ▷ emphasizing.
   ▷ stressing.
2. Repeat.

Check Yourself

Here are the most important expressions. Fill in each blank with an appropriate word. It is best to do this orally without writing in your book as you may want to check yourself again later.

You can use this page as an *aide memoire* while taking part in the Mini-Meetings.

Beginnings

1. I would _____ to _____ by . . .
2. I _____ like to _____ a few _____ concerning . . .
3. I _____ like to _____ on the problem of . . .
4. I would like to _____ _____ that . . .
5. There are three _____ I'd like to _____ .

Ordering

6. _____ of _____ , we must _____ in mind . . .
7. At the _____ . . .
8. To _____ with, . . .

Introducing a new point

9. I would _____ like to _____ briefly to the problem of . . .
10. The _____ issue I would like to _____ on is . . .

Adding

11. In _____ , . . .
12. I _____ add that . . .
13. As _____ as . . ., there is also . . .

Giving an example

14. _____ me _____ an example . . .
15. To _____ this _____ , let us consider . . .
16. A _____ in point is . . .

Balancing

17. On the one _____ . . ., but on the _____ hand . . .
18. _____ . . ., we mustn't forget . . .
19. _____ . . ., we have to remember . . .

Generalising

20. On the _____ , . . .
21. _____ speaking, . . .
22. _____ and large, . . .

Stating preferences

23. I _____ to favour . . . as opposed to . . .
24. I _____ rather . . . than . . .

Concluding

25. _____ me conclude _____ saying . . .
26. I'd like to _____ by _____ that . . .

Mini-Meeting 1

PART 1 Work in groups of 2. Think of a subject about which you can talk without too much difficulty. Now you should present your argument using at least one phrase from each of the sections above. You may do the functions in any order you want. Your partner will not interrupt, but he/she will put a tick in the box provided every time you use one of the phrases correctly.

Remember you are practising the *language of meetings* — don't worry too much about the content of what you say! If you like, you can use the ideas given below.

PART 2 Change roles and repeat the exercise.
PART 3 Change partners but keep the same subject and repeat the exercise.

STUDENT A   STUDENT B

	1st time	2nd time	3rd time
BEGINNING			
ORDERING			
INTRODUCING A NEW POINT			
ADDING			
GIVING AN EXAMPLE			
BALANCING			
GENERALISING			
STATING PREFERENCES			
CONCLUDING			

Euthanasia

Murder
Often a cure
Modern medicine progresses fast
Who does it?

Mercy killing
Human vegetable
The right to die
Better than unbearable pain

Saving Money

Savings give you freedom
Responsibility for family
Future problem — "for a rainy day"
Better retirement

Might die tomorrow
Live now, pay later
Why let others waste it later?
Socially irresponsible

> *Most managers talk for 80%
> of the time during meetings
> and then thank everybody for
> their contributions.*

> *Skill at negotiations is
> essential to the manager. It
> can mean life or death for his
> career.*

> *If you explain so clearly that
> nobody can misunderstand,
> somebody will.*

Mini-Meeting 2

PART 1 Think of a one word subject, your own, or one of those suggested below, write your subject on a small piece of paper and give it to your teacher. Your teacher will then mix up the papers and give one to each student. The object of the exercise is to talk on this subject for 60 seconds using as many of the phrases for **Presenting an Argument** as you can. You have one minute to prepare your talk. Then form pairs and give your talk to your partner. When you've finished, change roles.

PART 2 Change partners and subjects.

PART 3 Think of a new subject and repeat the exercise but now you should talk for 2 minutes.

Possible subjects

Money	**Children**	**Onions**
Death	**Marriage**	**Research**
Banking	**Management**	**Aid**

Match and Complete 1

face	the deal	_____
run	the options	_____
close	a suggestion	_____
put forward	the problem	_____
weigh	a meeting	_____

1. What a way to _____! Nobody was given a chance to say anything.
2. We have to _____ before we make a decision.
3. Did you _____ with Hall? Is it all signed and sealed?
4. When you have to _____ of middle age, you won't laugh like that.
5. Every time I _____, I get jumped on.

Match and Complete 2

an overall	step	_____
a short-term	point	_____
a hasty	picture	_____
a preliminary	decision	_____
a moot	solution	_____

1. We shouldn't be forced into a _____ on this; given its importance we must think it over carefully.
2. As a _____ we would be prepared to exchange certain general information and perhaps later we will be able to move on to more important things.
3. That's a _____ and we shouldn't accept it as being true without discussing it further.
4. That's a good _____ but we still need something more lasting for the future.
5. Margaret, you've been here longer than anyone. Ignoring the details, can you give us the _____ as you see it?

Match and Complete 3

miss	an example	_____
give	a setback	_____
pose	the point	_____
hammer out	a compromise	_____
suffer	a problem	_____

1. Even if it takes 2 months, we'll _____.

2. It was unlucky to _____ like that; there was an unexpected change in government and now we'll have to wait an additional 3 months.

3. I think you _____, Bill. He didn't say that he was opposed to the scheme: he just said it wasn't as good as it could be.

4. I hope the change in dates won't _____ for you.

5. Could you _____ of what you mean?

Match and Complete 4

Which prepositions go in the following expressions?

of   on   in   to

_____	account	_____
_____	addition	_____
_____	the agenda	
_____	agreement	_____
_____	the basis	_____

1. I think we're all _____ that.

2. What's _____ for today?

3. _____ this report, I think we can go ahead with our plans.

4. I'm afraid we'll have to cancel the order _____ the cost.

5. _____ his age, there is also the fact that he doesn't speak German.

Match and Complete 5

Which prepositions go in the following expressions?

in   on   of   at

_____ **behalf** _____

_____ **best**

_____ **business**

_____ **business**

_____ **charge** _____

_____ **certain circumstances**

1. The boss is away _____ in France.
2. I can't remember who's _____ the publicity. Is it Hill or Lewis?
3. _____ my government I would like to thank you for the kindness you have shown us.
4. _____ I could see us accepting, but not in our current financial situation.
5. _____ we'll make 5000, I just can't see us doing any better than that.
6. They've been _____ for over thirty years.

"First of all, we'll discontinue the pills."

Discussion

Complete the questionaire individually and then discuss your answers together with the teacher.

1. When somebody is speaking, what do you do?   **In British culture**
In your culture
    Look at your papers
    Look at the person
    Look round the room
    Stare blankly into space

2. When you are speaking, where do you look?

                                     In British culture
In your culture
    At one particular person
    At your papers
    Generally at everybody present
    Into space

3. How do you show that you have finished talking?

                                     In British culture
In your culture
    By the words you use
    By sitting back in your chair
    By looking at the other people
    By looking away from other people

4. How can you interrupt someone who is speaking?

                                     In British culture
In your culture
    By raising a finger and waiting
    By jumping in at that moment
    By waiting until there is a pause
    By waiting until you are asked to speak

5. Which responses do you expect to see from other people when somebody is talking and what does each one signify?

                                     In British culture
In your culture
    Nodding of the head
    Shaking of the head
    Facial expressions
    Eye movements
    Gestures with the hands

Some suggestions for what is usual in British culture are given on page 127.

3 Opinions

Language Awareness

How do you:

1. Ask someone for their opinion?

_____

2. Ask someone for their reaction to what has been said?

_____

3. Give an opinion?

_____

Is your phrase strong, neutral or tentative?

4. Bring someone into the discussion to answer a question?

_____

5. Bring someone into the discussion to comment?

_____

6. Begin to summarize what has been said?

_____

Asking for an Opinion

What's your opinion of . . . ?

What's your 'position on . . . ?

What do you think of . . . ?

I'd like to hear your views on . . .

1. ▷ view.

Asking for a Reaction

Could I ask for your reaction to . . . ?

I was wondering where you 'stood on this question?

Where ²exactly do you 'stand on this issue?

I wonder if you'd like to comment, Mrs Lang?

1. Here "what is your point of view?"
2. Can show impatience.

Giving Strong Opinions

I 'firmly believe that . . .

I'm absolutely convinced that . . .

It's my belief that . . .

There's no doubt in my mind that . . .

It's ²quite ³clear that . . .

I'm ⁴certain that . . .

It's my ⁵considered opinion that . . .

1. Strongly.
   ▷ sincerely.
2. Here completely.
3. ▷ evident.
4. ▷ sure.
5. Suggests that you have thought a lot about the subject.

Giving Neutral Opinions

I ²think that . . .

In 'my ³opinion, . . .

It's 'my ³opinion that . . .

As 'I see it, . . .

As far as 'I'm concerned . . .

⁴From 'my point of view . . .

1. In all these phrases I/my/our is usually stressed.
2. ▷ believe — more formal.
   ▷ feel — less formal.
3. ▷ view.
4. Note the preposition: *from my point of view*, but *in my view*.

Giving Tentative Opinions

It 'seems to me that . . .

I ²would say that . . .

As far as I'm able to ³judge . . .

I think it ²would be fair to say that . . .

1. ▷ would seem — more formal.
2. Using *would* gives more flexibility in case you need to change your view later. It is diplomatic and avoids offending the listener(s) (See page 10).
3. Here form an opinion.

Bringing in to Answer a Question

I'd like to ask my colleague Ms Davis to give us her views on that.

If I may, I'd like to ask my colleague Mrs Wang to reply to that.

I think Mr Doll is more qualified than I am to deal with this question.

I would like to bring in Ms Short who has studied this matter in more [1]detail than I have.

Perhaps Mr Bird would [2]care to answer that.

1. No "s" at the end of *detail*: it is part of the phrase *in detail*.
2. ▷ like.

Bringing in to Present a Point

Ms Sheppard, would you like to come in here?

Allow me to [1]give the floor to Ms Redgrave.

I would like to invite Mr Wells to present his views on . . .

I'd like to call [2]on Mrs Kelly to present her views on . . .

Mr Right, would you care to comment?

I think Mr Douglas would like to make a point.

1. Give permission to speak.
2. ▷ upon — more formal.

Summarizing

Well, if I could just sum up the discussion . . .

To summarize, I think we are in agreement on . . .

To sum up, there seems to be . . .

In short, . . .

Briefly, the main points that have been made are . . .

Well, at this [1]stage I feel I should summarize the matter as it [2]stands . . .

If I may just [3]go over the main points [4]raised so far?

1. ▷ point.
   ▷ juncture.
2. After all that has been said so far.
3. Repeat.
4. Short for "the main points which have been raised."

Check Yourself

Here are the most important expressions. Fill in each blank with an appropriate word. It is best to do this orally without writing in your book as you may want to check yourself again later.

You can use this page as an *aide memoire* while taking part in the Mini-Meetings.

Asking for an opinion

1. What's your _____ of . . . ?
2. What's your _____ on . . . ?
3. What do you _____ of . . . ?
4. I'd like to _____ your views on . . .

Asking for a reaction

5. Could I ask for your _____ to . . . ?
6. I was _____ where you _____ on this question?
7. Where _____ do you _____ on this issue?
8. I _____ if you'd _____ to _____, Mrs Lang?

Giving strong opinions

9. I _____ believe that . . .
10. I'm absolutely _____ that . . .
11. There's no _____ in my _____ that . . .

Giving neutral opinions

12. I _____ that . . .
13. As _____ as I'm _____ . . .
14. _____ my _____ of view . . .

Giving tentative opinions

15. It _____ to me that . . .
16. I would _____ that . . .
17. As _____ as I'm able to _____ . . .

Bringing in to answer a question

18. I'd like to _____ my _____ Ms Davis to _____ us her _____ on that.
19. If I _____, I'd like to _____ my _____ Mrs Wang to _____ to that.
20. I think Mr Doll is more _____ _____ I am to _____ with this _____.

Bringing in to present a point

21. Ms Sheppard, _____ you like to _____ in _____?
22. _____ me to _____ the _____ to Ms Redgrave.
23. I would like to _____ Mr Wells to _____ his views _____ . . .

Summarizing

24. _____, if I could _____ sum _____ the discussion . . .
25. Well, at this _____ I feel I should _____ the matter as it _____ . . .
26. If I may just go _____ the main points _____ so far?

Mini-Meeting 1

PART 1 Work in groups of 3. Ask your partner for his/her opinion on any subject that comes to mind. Be prepared to give your own opinion as well. Do not get involved in long discussions as the object of the exercise is to practise the phrases as much as possible.

PART 2 Change roles and repeat the exercise. If you run out of ideas, feel free to use the topic below — or any other from elsewhere in the book. Usually language is about *content*, but remember you are practising the important language of meetings, and the subject matter is less important than becoming fluent in the *language of meetings*.

PART 3 Change partners but keep the same subjects and repeat the exercise.

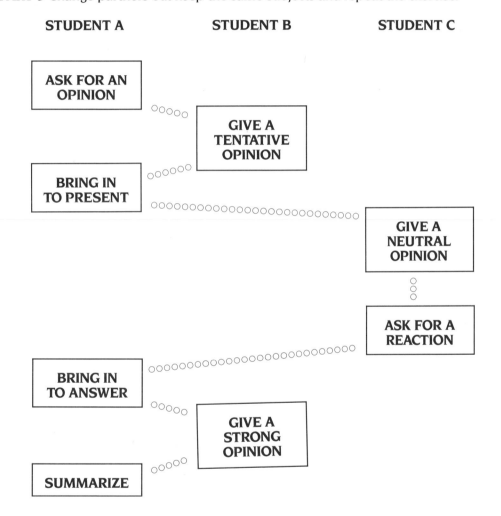

English as a World Language

Already is
Richest of world's languages
Shakespeare
Most flexible

Cultural domination
Goethe, Dante, Molière
Not clear, accurate, philosophical
Esperanto easier to learn

> A *conference should consist of* 3 men, two of whom are absent.

> When you are right no one remembers; when you are wrong no one forgets.

> A committee is twelve men doing the work of one.

Mini-Meeting 2

PART 1 In groups of 3, briefly discuss the following list of subjects. At the end of your short discussion take it in turns to summarize what has been said.

1 Pop music
2 Sunbathing
3 Cooking
4 Keeping fit
5 Gardening
6 Monarchies
7 Private education
8 Hire Purchase
9 Fast food
10 Computers

PART 2 Now change partners and repeat the exercise.

Match and Complete 1

express	the matter	_____
raise	a role	_____
reach	a conclusion	_____
make	an opinion	_____
play	an effort	_____

1. I'll _____ with Finance as soon as I get a chance.
2. Prices obviously _____, but they're not the only factor.
3. If we all _____, we could double our profits.
4. Every time I _____ he interrupts me.
5. Can you _____ about the Giva Dam Project yet?

Match and Complete 2

a workable	misunderstanding	_____
a dominant	solution	_____
a slight	factor	_____
a fruitful	opinion	_____
a considered	discussion	_____

1. We seem to have arrived at _____ and I can't see any serious difficulties arising in the near future.
2. There seems to be a _____. I said 60 thousand, not 16 thousand.
3. It is our _____ that this merger will be beneficial to both parties.
4. Thank you for coming today and I hope we will be able to have _____ _____ on the merits of the various projects.
5. _____ in my decision was the expense involved.

Match and Complete 3

see	(your) support to . . .	_____
answer	(your) opinion of	_____
set	(your) question	_____
share	(your) mind(s) at rest	_____
lend	(your) point	_____

1. I'm afraid I can't _____ until I've spoken to my Head Office.
2. I can't say that I _____ his ability; I don't think he's very capable.
3. Let me _____ on that. I can promise you that the project will be completed on time.
4. I _____, but I still think that . . .
5. If you could _____ the scheme, I'm sure the others would accept it.

Match and Complete 4

Which prepositions go in the following expressions?

with   in   under

_____ **no circumstances**

_____ **common**

_____ **conclusion**

_____ **concrete terms**

_____ **conjunction** _____

1. _____ could we accept such a low offer.
2. _____, we are offering you a salary of £20,000 a year plus car.
3. Let me say, _____, that it has been a pleasure to work with such a dedicated group of people.
4. Our companies have a lot _____. They're both old established firms and both need some new blood.
5. This loan, _____ the fall in the dollar, should save us from bankruptcy.

Match and Complete 5

Which prepositions go in the following expressions?

at   under   with   on   in

_____ **connection** _____

_____ **consideration**

_____ **the contrary**

_____ **all costs**

_____**cross purposes**

1. I don't think the boss is too old. _____, I think he has quite a few years left in him.
2. We must get this contract _____. If we don't, we're never going to be able to survive.
3. The meeting is _____ the proposed extension.
4. Your candidature is _____ Dr Rogers. I can't tell you any more than that.
5. We seem to be talking _____.

"Now, for an opposing viewpoint, here's my wife."

Discussion

Are you a good negotiator? Fill in this questionnaire individually, then compare your answers with the others in your group.

The Good Negotiator

Put the following qualities in order of importance. Number the *most* important for you 1, the next 2, down to 10 for the factor you consider *least* important.

- ☐ Expresses him/herself well.
- ☐ Is sensitive to body language.
- ☐ Is a good listener.
- ☐ Prepares well beforehand.
- ☐ Works well under pressure.
- ☐ Never shows annoyance or anger.
- ☐ Is able to say nothing very convincingly.
- ☐ Asks the right questions.
- ☐ Deals well with difficult questions.
- ☐ Can say "I don't understand that" five times after five explanations.

What other qualities can you think of for a good negotiator?
Which, if any, do you think you need to improve yourself?

4 Agreeing and Disagreeing

Language Awareness

How do you:

1. Say you agree with someone?

_____

Is your phrase acceptable in all situations?

2. Say you agree but . . .

_____

3. Say you disagree?

_____

Is your phrase strong, neutral or tactful?

4. Say you disagree but . . .

_____

5. How you can make your disagreement more acceptable?

_____

Strong Agreement

I [1]completely agree.
I agree entirely with your point of view.
[2]I'm of exactly the same opinion.
I'm in [3]total [4]agreement.

1. ▷ thoroughly.
   ▷ entirely
2. I have.
3. ▷ complete.
4. ▷ accord — very formal.

Neutral Agreement

I agree.
I think we are in agreement on that.
I think you're right.
I think we [1]can accept your position on that.

1. ▷ could — less certain.

Partial Agreement

[1]I would tend to agree with you on that.
I agree with you on the [2]whole, but it could be said
   that . . .
I agree in [3]principle, but . . .
[4]By and large I would accept your views, but . . .
Although I agree with most of what you've said, I find
   it difficult to agree with your point about . . .

1. Shows agreement but still leaves room
   for manoeuvre. Often followed by a
   "but . . .".
2. Taking everything into consideration.
3. In general, usually followed by giving
   the *details* on which you still disagree,
   or where you need more information.
4. To a great extent.

Softening Strong Disagreement

[1]Frankly, . . .
[1]To be quite frank, . . .
To put it [2]bluntly, . . .
[3]With respect, . . .

Strong disagreement is relatively rare in
English. Often introduced by various
"softeners" before phrases of strong
disagreement. Any of the phrases for
"softening" may be used before any of
the phrases for Strong Disagreement.
1. These are ways of showing your
   thoughts and feelings clearly and
   honestly.
2. Directly — without wasting time being
   unnecessarily diplomatic about it.
3. ▷ With due respect — more formal.
   ▷ With all due respect — even more
   formal.

Strong Disagreement

I [1]totally disagree with you.

[2]I don't agree at all.

You're completely mistaken.

I disagree entirely.

[3]Under no circumstances could I agree to that.

What you are saying is just not [4]feasible.

1. ▷ completely.
   ▷ wholly.
   ▷ utterly — only used in this negative way
2. Not as strong as *disagree* (see page 13).
3. After *under no circumstances* the auxiliary and the subject are inverted.
4. ▷ possible.

Softening Neutral Disagreement

[1]I'm afraid . . .

[1]I'm sorry, . . .

With respect, . . .

I respect your opinion, of course, however . . .

Similar to Softening Strong Disagreement except that you not so obliged to use these phrases with Neutral Disagreement. It is, however, a good idea to "soften" any disagreement in English.

1. These two phrases are included here and not in Softening Strong Disagreement as they are not as powerful as the other phrases. (see page 12).

Neutral Disagreement

I don't [1]completely agree with you on that.

I really can't agree with you on that.

I can't say that I share your view.

[2]We'll have to agree to differ.

I'm not [1]totally convinced by your argument.

I can't accept your point of view.

I can't help feeling that . . .

I feel I must disagree.

I really must take [3]issue with you here.

1. Although this suggests you agree to a large extent, it usually means the contrary.
2. A convenient way to stop the argument if there doesn't seem to be any way to reach agreement on the subject.
3. Argue.

Tactful Disagreement

I agree up to a point, but . . .

To a certain extent I agree with you, but . . .

You have a point there, but . . .

I [1]take your point, Mr Hoffman, but have you considered . . .?

I can see your point of view, but surely . . .

I have some sympathy with your [2]position, but . . .

The main difference between this section and Partial Agreement is that these phrases are on the negative side. They suggest below 50% agreement, whereas the phrases in Partial Agreement suggest agreement above 50%.
1. ▷ see.
2. ▷ argument.
   ▷ view.

Check Yourself

Here are the most important expressions. Fill in each blank with an appropriate word. It is best to do this orally without writing in your book as you may want to check yourself again later.

You can use this page as an *aide memoire* while taking part in the Mini-Meetings.

Strong agreement

1. I _____ agree.
2. I agree _____ with your _____ of _____.
3. I'm of _____ the same _____.
4. I'm in _____ _____.

Neutral agreement

5. I think we are in _____ _____ that.
6. I think we can _____ your _____ on that.

Partial agreement

7. I _____ _____ to agree with you on that.
8. I agree with you on the _____, but it _____ be said that . . .
9. By and _____ I would _____ your views, but . . .
10. _____ I agree with _____ of what you've said, I _____ it difficult to agree with your _____ about . . .

Softening strong disagreement

11. _____, . . .
12. To be _____ frank, . . .
13. To _____ it _____, . . .

Strong disagreement

14. I _____ disagree with you.
15. _____ no _____ could I agree to that.
16. What you are _____ is just not _____.

Softening neutral disagreement

17. I'm _____ . . .
18. _____ respect, . . .
19. I _____ your opinion, of _____; however . . .

Neutral disagreement

20. I don't _____ agree with you _____ that.
21. I really _____ agree with you _____ that.
22. I can't _____ that I _____ your view.
23. We'll _____ to agree to _____.
24. I _____ must _____ issue _____ you here.

Tactful disagreement

25. I _____ up to a _____, but . . .
26. To a _____ _____ I agree with you, but . . .
27. I have some _____ with your _____, but . . .

Mini-Meeting 1

PART 1 Work in groups of 3. Think of two subjects about which you can give fairly extreme opinions. When you've finished your first subject, change roles with your partners. Keep changing roles until all the subjects are finished.

PART 2 Change groups but use the same subjects.

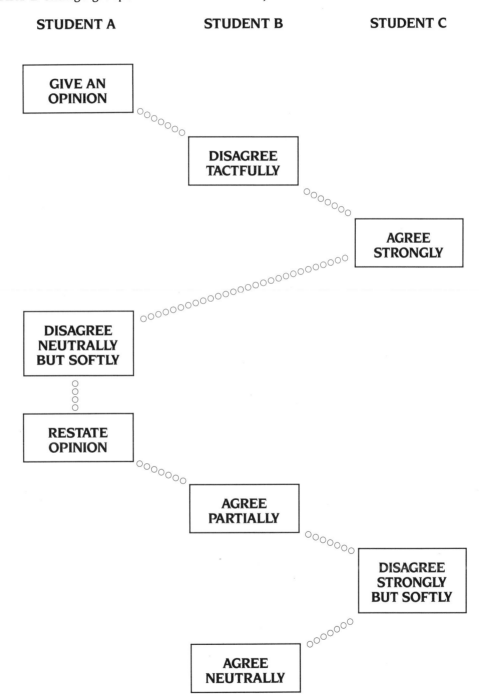

STUDENT A	STUDENT B	STUDENT C

GIVE AN OPINION

DISAGREE TACTFULLY

AGREE STRONGLY

DISAGREE NEUTRALLY BUT SOFTLY

RESTATE OPINION

AGREE PARTIALLY

DISAGREE STRONGLY BUT SOFTLY

AGREE NEUTRALLY

> There are two sides to every question: my side and the wrong side.

> We like a man to come right out and say what he thinks — if we agree with him.

> My idea of an agreeable person is a person who agrees with me.

Nuclear Weapons

Danger of accidents
Waste of money, thousands starving
Threaten our existence
Encourage war

Maintains balance of power
Disarmament unrealistic
Reduce possibility of global conflict
Can't 'undiscover' something

Computers

Time saver
Fewer staff
Create opportunities
As cheap as a typewriter

Time waster
Impersonal
Bought without thought
Do what manufacturers want, not what customers want

Mini-Meeting 2

Work in groups of 3 or 4. Take it in turns to give your opinions about the following subjects. The other students should agree or disagree.

1. Cats or dogs.
2. Football or tennis.
3. Bach or Beethoven.
4. Plastic or real flowers.
5. Honesty or diplomacy.
6. One piece swimming suits or bikinis.
7. The cinema or television.
8. Fame or anonymity.
9. Beauty or intelligence.
10. Fact or fiction.

When you've finished, change partners and repeat the exercise.

Match and Complete 1

take   hairs   _____

get   negotiations   _____

break off   resources   _____

allocate   results   _____

split   steps   _____

1. We won't get any money; they've said they won't _____ for this project.
2. Let's not _____; a difference of 1% is negligible and not worth worrying about.
3. If you are not more reasonable, we'll be forced to _____.
4. If you don't _____, you don't get paid.
5. If we don't_____ to increase efficiency, we'll have to close down.

Match and Complete 2

broad   factors   _____

wide-ranging   knowledge   _____

common   talks   _____

far-reaching   agreement   _____

various   repercussions   _____

1. There are _____ involved, not just the cost.
2. I think we are in_____on that and I don't think we need to go into the details at the present time.
3. The two negotiators said that their_____ had brought their countries closer together.
4. The company's decision to move out of the country rather than be nationalized has had _____: many governments now think twice about nationalization.
5. It was_____that the company had made a loss: somebody has been talking and now everybody knows about it.

Match and Complete 3

air	**(our) best**	_____
express	**(our) thanks**	_____
put	**(our) options open**	_____
do	**(our) cards on the table**	_____
keep	**(our) views**	_____

1. I'd like to _____ for the co-operation you've shown. Thank you.
2. Let's _____. We can go to 8,000 and not a penny more. What about you?
3. We can't guarantee anything, but we'll _____.
4. I'm glad we had this opportunity to _____ and even if we can't agree, at least we understand each other better.
5. Never agree or disagree immediately: you should always _____.

Match and Complete 4

a short	**basis**	_____
a key	**venture**	_____
a slight	**element**	_____
a joint	**disagreement**	_____
a reasonable	**adjournment**	_____

1. The project would be a _____. The idea is that we work together as partners.
2. A _____ in the success of the company was its ability to change with the times.
3. I think this would be a good moment to have a _____ _____. Shall we say 15 minutes?
4. That strikes me as a _____ for discussion.
5. I had a _____ with the boss yesterday; it wasn't over anything serious though.

Match and Complete 5

Which prepositions go in the following expressions?

for   under   in   to   into

_____ **detail**

_____ **discussion**

_____ **due course**

_____ **exchange** _____

_____ **some extent**

_____ **fact**

1. _____, the problem is bigger than we anticipated.

2. We could give you a reduction _____ permission to use your name in adverts.

3. The subject _____ is most important for the future of our company.

4. Don't worry, the problem will solve itself _____.

5. I agree with you _____, but I still can't understand why it's so urgent.

6. Don't go _____, keep it simple and clear.

"US and Soviet officials agreed on five adjectives to describe the meeting –
interesting, useful, frank, businesslike, productive –
but failed to agree on any prepositions."

Discussion

The Negotiating Process

Anyone observing or participating in negotiations for the first time cannot fail to be struck by the ritual of it all. Indeed, if the participants themselves were not so serious and the issues at stake so important, the set-up might have its amusing side. For there may be as many as 20 or 30 people sitting at either side of a large table and yet for long periods it seems that one person from each side is actually speaking. Usually they are extremely polite and formal; they speak slowly and deliberately, and their language is full of rhetoric. From time to time there are outbursts of anger, with appeals for voiceless support from the other members of their party. But it is often difficult to believe that they are genuine. One makes a point and then the other responds. Some points seem hardly relevant to the issues or problems which appear on the agenda but they are continually hit backwards and forwards with the monotony of a long rally on the Centre Court at Wimbledon. The repetition, like the meeting, seems to be endless. The only respite is afforded by the adjournments which seem to increase in number as the meeting progresses. After each adjournment, it is as if the meeting begins afresh. If the observer is listening attentively he will realize that some of the stronger statements have now been watered down; and offers and claims which were 'final' have been imperceptibly adjusted. Gradually many of the points fall by the wayside. The end often comes suddenly although sometimes it is difficult to see why, since nothing firm seems to have been agreed. The meeting breaks up and people shake hands.

From *Negotiating in Practice* by K. Sisson, Institute of Personnel Management Publications

Does this seem to be a realistic example of a meeting?
Would the description above fit meetings in your country?

5 Interrupting

I'M SORRY TO INTERRUPT, BUT...

Language Awareness

How do you:

1. Interrupt someone?

_____

Is your phrase acceptable in all situations?

2. Say that you want to say something?

_____

3. Say that you want to comment on what someone has said?

_____

4. Return to the subject after an interruption?

_____

5. Stop someone interrupting you?

_____

Is your phrase offensive?

6. Reduce the chance of someone interrupting you?

_____

Interrupting

May I interrupt you for a [1]moment?

Sorry to [2]interrupt, but . . .

If I may just interrupt you for a [1]moment,
I'd like to . . .

I don't want to interrupt, but . . .

This is acceptable when the interruption is made at the right moment, i.e. during a pause in what the speaker is saying. This may be when the speaker hesitates or when he/she is changing from one subject to another. To interrupt somebody in mid-sentence is normally impolite.

1. Suggests that you are not going to talk for a long time. This makes your interruption more acceptable.
2. ▷ break in — less formal.

Taking the Floor

[1]Could I come in at this point?

[1]Could I say something about . . . ?

If I [1]could just come in here . . . ?

If no one [2]objects, I'd like to say a few words
about . . .

If I [1]could say a word about . . .

I have a point to [3]make here.

1. ▷ can — informal.
   ▷ may — more formal.
   ▷ might — even more formal.
2. It is unlikely that anyone will object.
3. ▷ raise.

Commenting

I wonder if I [1]could comment on that last point?

Excuse me, but I'd just like to point out that . . .

I'd like to add something here, if I may?

May I just draw your attention to the fact that . . .

Excuse me, but I think it's relevant to add that . . .

Before we go any further, may I point out . . .

These are all phrases which introduce a comment. A comment is normally short and relevant to what the speaker has just said.

1. ▷ might — more formal.

Coming Back to a Point

As I was saying . . .

¹Coming back to what I was saying . . .

Perhaps I could ²resume . . .

If I may just go back to the point I was making . . .

If I ³could continue . . .

⁴Your question leads us back to . . .

To return to . . .

Many interruptions are clarifications and as soon as you have given the necessary information, you return to what you were saying by using one of these phrases.
1. ▷ Going.
2. Continue after being interrupted.
3. ▷ may.
4. This is sometimes used even if the question has nothing to do with the subject.

Preventing an Interruption

Perhaps I could ¹return to that point later on . . .

If I ²might just finish . . .

With your permission, I'd rather finish what I was saying.

³With respect, I should like to finish the point I was making . . .

If you would allow me to continue . . .

⁴If you would be so kind as to let me finish . . .

All of these can be impolite, but so can many interruptions. It very often depends on the intonation you use. Don't be sarcastic.
1. This does not necessarily mean that you will.
2. ▷ could — less formal.
   ▷ can — even less formal.
3. This allows you to be a little impolite. It is the sort of phrase you could use when you want to disagree with your boss. Some bosses could be offended by a phrase such as I *disagree*; however, if you say *With respect* I *disagree*, it is less likely that he/she will be offended.
4. Too formal expression, this easily gives an impression of rudeness.

Pre-empting an Interruption

There are ¹two points I would like to make.

First, I would like to reply to Mr Hawk and then I would like to comment on . . .

²Very briefly, . . .

I'd ³just like to . . .

These are ways of making it difficult for someone to interrupt you. They are used at the beginning of what you want to say.
1. Mentioning the number of points makes it very difficult for someone to interrupt you.
   ▷ several.
2. Even if you are not brief, this phrase should allow you to keep the floor.
3. Suggests you are only going to talk for a short time.

Check Yourself

Here are the most important expressions. Fill in each blank with an appropriate word. It is best to do this orally without writing in your book as you may want to check yourself again later.

You can use this page as an *aide memoire* while taking part in the Mini-Meetings.

Interrupting

1. _____ I _____ you for a moment?
2. _____ to _____, but . . .
3. If I may _____ _____ you for a _____, I'd like to . . .
4. I _____ want to _____ but . . .

Taking the floor

5. _____ I _____ in at this _____?
6. _____ I say _____ about . . .?
7. If I _____ _____ come _____ here . . .
8. If no one _____, I'd like to say a _____ _____ about . . .
9. If I could _____ a _____ about . . .
10. I have a _____ to _____ here.

Commenting

11. I _____ if I _____ _____ on that last point?
12. _____ me, but I'd _____ like to point _____ that . . .
13. I'd like to _____ something _____ , if I _____?
14. May I just _____ your _____ to the fact that . . .
15. Excuse me, but I _____ it's _____ to add that . . .
16. _____ we go any _____, may I _____ out . . .

Coming back to a point

17. _____ I was _____ . . .
18. _____ back to what I was _____ . . .
19. Perhaps I could _____ . . .
20. If I may just _____ _____ to the point I was _____ . . .
21. Your question _____ us _____ to . . .
22. To _____ to . . .

Preventing an interruption

23. Perhaps I could _____ to that point _____ on . . .
24. If I _____ just _____ . . .
25. With your _____, I'd _____ finish what I was saying.
26. With _____, I should like to _____ the point I was _____ . . .
27. If you _____ _____ me to continue . . .
28. If you would be _____ kind _____ to _____ me finish . . .

Pre-empting an interruption

29. There are _____ _____ I would like to _____ . . .
30. Very _____, . . .

Mini-Meeting 1

PART 1 Work in groups of 2. Think of two subjects you can talk about without having to think too much. When you've finished your first subject, change roles with your partner. Then change roles again until all four subjects are finished.

PART 2 Change partners but use the same subjects.

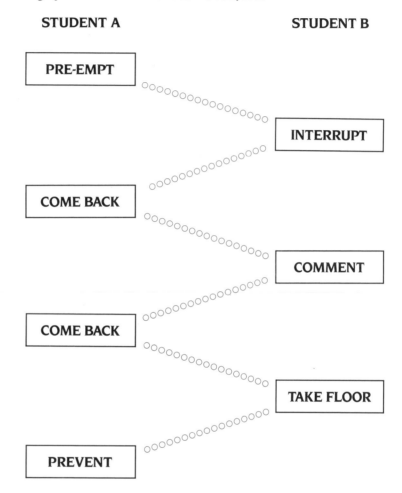

STUDENT A   STUDENT B

PRE-EMPT

INTERRUPT

COME BACK

COMMENT

COME BACK

TAKE FLOOR

PREVENT

Drinking

Social habit	Alcoholics often aggressive
Enjoyable	Drinking and driving
Helps shy people	Religious offence to some
Matter for individual choice	Addictive

Qualifications

Objective test of competence	Paper qualifications
Provide motivation	Don't reflect ability
No other system	Nervous people
Usually mean something	Experience better

> Don't say yes until I've
> finished talking.

> It is not necessary to
> understand things in order to
> argue about them.

> Say no, then negotiate.

Mini-Meeting 2

PART 1 Your teacher is going to give a short talk on the history of language teaching; you are asked to interrupt as often as possible.

PART 2 Now choose a subject, about which you are reasonably well informed, and prepare a short talk on it. When you are ready, get into groups of 3 and follow the same procedure as in PART 1. You should reply to the questions asked as briefly as possible.

Mini-Meeting 3

PART 1 Work in groups of 3. One student chooses a subject and starts talking about it; the other students try to interrupt and continue talking about the same subject. Be careful to interrupt only when there's a pause.

PART 2 Change roles until everybody has had a turn.

Reminder

The topics you choose are not important. You are practising the language of meetings — **any** meetings, so feel free to choose serious topics about your job, or more light-hearted topics, such as some of those suggested in this book. The important thing is to practise the *language of meetings*.

Match and Complete 1

face	**a word**	_____
have	**a deal**	_____
say	**the deadlock**	_____
make	**the know-how**	_____
break	**the facts**	_____

1. Can I just _____ on that?
2. I don't think she _____ , she's too young, too inexperienced.
3. We have to _____ , we simply don't have enough money to consider expanding at the moment.
4. There must be a way to _____. What can we offer them?
5. Let's _____. I'll drop the price a little, if you increase your order.

Match and Complete 2

a fruitful	**outlook**	_____
a ready-made	**matter**	_____
a narrow	**association**	_____
a firm	**solution**	_____
a straightforward	**commitment**	_____

1. May I just say I think this is a _____ and it shouldn't take long to decide.
2. I think we can look forward to a _____ with this Japanese company.
3. Sorry to butt in, but I think that's a rather _____.
4. There is no _____ to our problems.
5. If we don't make a _____ soon, we'll lose the contract.

Match and Complete 3

deal with	a mistake	_____
rule out	the difficulty	_____
overcome	the discussion	_____
make	the possibility	_____
wind up	the problem	_____

1. It's 5 o'clock — time to _____ and go home, I'm afraid.
2. Let John _____; after all, he's in charge.
3. We can't _____ that they have another customer. I say we pay what they're asking.
4. I hope we don't _____ buying these shares.
5. If we can _____ of production costs, I think we have a winner.

Match and Complete 4

Which prepositions go in the following expressions?

                    of   at   in

          _____ favour _____

          _____ this field

          _____ (my) fingertips

          _____ first sight

          _____ general

1. I think it's a great idea; I'm _____ it.
2. I'm sorry, I don't have that information _____.
   I'll ask Richard to come in, he's more familiar with it than I am.
3. _____ I'd say no. The offer isn't good enough. Of course I'll have to study it in more detail before we give a definitive answer.
4. _____ more people watch television than read newspapers.
5. She's the best there is _____. She's more qualified and more experienced than anyone else.

Match and Complete 5

Which prepositions go in the following expressions?

under   on   in   to   with

_____ **good terms** _____

_____ **hand**

_____ **(your) own interest**

_____ **no illusions**

_____ **the impression that . . .**

1. I should be able to help you there — we've been _____ them for years.
2. It would be _____ to accept the promotion.
3. You should be _____ as to who is the boss around here. He may be the Director, but I run the place.
4. I don't have the figures _____. Can I call you back in half an hour?
5. I was _____ you had the power to decide.

*"Pardon me for interrupting, Mr Wertenbaker,
but aren't you going to apologise for keeping me
on hold for two hours and seventeen minutes?"*

Discussion

HOW TO SURVIVE A BORING MEETING

Here are some of the tried and tested ways of keeping your sanity and avoiding falling sleep during the sort of meeting you wouldn't wish on your worst friend.

1. Imagine the Chairman or Chairwoman with no clothes.
2. Start a lottery for the time the meeting will finish.
3. Write a love poem.
4. Write a shopping list for the next six months.
5. Catch up on all your correspondence — remember to look up occasionally.
6. Photocopy the next 50 pages of the novel you are reading and put them between the pages of a report.
7. Fantasize about what absent members are doing.
8. Philosophize as follows: Am I really sitting here in this meeting? Is this all there is to existence?
9. Draw caricatures of the members you hate.
10. Note one of the favourite phrases of the Chairman/Chairwoman or any other verbose speaker and count how many times he/she uses it.
11. Pick a vogue word like, "transparent" and count how many times it comes up.
12. Send a note to someone who came late saying, "Pity you weren't here to defend yourself".
13. Ask one or all of the following questions:
    But is this really relevant?
    But isn't this only the tip of the iceberg?
    May I play the devil's advocate for a moment?
    Could we adjourn the meeting for a few minutes?

Which, if any, of the above have you tried?
How do *you* survive boring meetings — share your good ideas!

6 Clarifying

Language Awareness

How do you:

1. Check what someone has said?

_____

Is your phrase too direct?

2. Ask someone to repeat what they've said?

_____

Is your phrase acceptable in all situations?

3. Tell someone they haven't understood you?

_____

Is your phrase diplomatic enough?

4. Say you're going to repeat yourself in different words?

_____

Asking for Confirmation

¹**Would I be ²correct in saying that . . . ?**

If I've understood you correctly, you're saying that . . . ?

¹**Correct me if I'm wrong, but . . .**

¹**Am I ²correct in assuming that . . . ?**

When you say . . ., do you mean that . . . ?

Are you saying that . . . ?

³**Basically, what you're saying is . . .**

One way of avoiding misunderstandings is by checking what someone has said. It is very difficult to react in an appropriate way if you are not clear about what has been said. It is also important in that, by rephrasing their position, you show that you have not only listened to them, but also that you attach importance to what they have said.

1. This invites a correction and therefore shows your openness.
2. ▷ right.
3. Can show impatience, especially if the previous speaker was not very clear.

Asking for a Repetition

I'm afraid I'm not ¹quite clear what you mean by that.

I'm sorry, I didn't ¹quite ²follow what you said about . . .

I'm afraid I don't understand what you mean.

I'm afraid I didn't ¹quite ³get your last point. Could you go over it again please?

Helps in three ways:

a. if you don't understand someone who is not clear, but it is impolite to say so.
b. if you don't understand because of your or the speaker's limitations in English — a repetition gives you another chance to understand.
c. if you **have** understood, but need time to think.

1. Completely. Suggests you've understood nearly everything when, in fact, you may have understood very little.
2. ▷ catch.
   ▷ understand.
   ▷ get.
3. ▷ understand.
   ▷ catch.

Correcting Misunderstandings

I'm afraid there seems to have been a [1]slight misunderstanding.

[2]We seem to be talking at cross purposes.

I think you've misunderstood me.

That isn't quite what I meant.

[3]With respect, that is not what I said.

All of these phrases would normally be followed by a phrase from re-phrasing below.

1. Suggests there has not been a "complete" misunderstanding (see page 12).
   ▷ some.
2. This is used when someone has misunderstood you and has reacted to his/her impression of what you said.
3. Even though you are using the phrase "with respect", you should still be careful not to offend.

Re-phrasing

Perhaps I haven't made myself clear. [1]Basically, what I'm trying to say is . . .

Sorry, I'm probably not making myself clear. Let me put it another way . . .

Perhaps I should make that clearer by saying . . .

Allow me to rephrase that.

To be more specific, . . .

Put simply, . . .

These phrases can either be used in reply to a request for clarification, or as a way of reinforcing your point by putting it in other words. Notice that it is more polite and diplomatic to say that it is your fault even if it isn't. Avoid phrases like *You didn't understand*.

1. *Here* means you are attempting a simplification of your previous point.

Check Yourself

Here are the most important expressions. Fill in each blank with an appropriate word. It is best to do this orally without writing in your book as you may want to check yourself again later.

You can use this page as an *aide memoire* while taking part in the Mini-Meetings.

Asking for confirmation

1. _____ I be _____ in saying that . . .
2. If I've _____ you _____, you're saying that . . .
3. _____ me if I'm _____, but . . .
4. Am I _____ in _____ that . . .
5. _____ you say . . . . ., do you _____ that . . .
6. Are you _____ that . . .
7. _____, what you're _____ is . . .

Asking for a repetition

8. I'm afraid I'm not _____ clear what you _____ by that.
9. I'm sorry, I didn't _____ _____ what you said about . . .
10. I'm _____ I don't _____ what you mean.
11. I'm afraid I didn't _____ _____ your last point. Could you _____ _____ it again please?

Correcting misunderstandings

12. I'm afraid _____ seems to have been a _____ _____.
13. We seem to be _____ at _____ purposes.
14. I think you've _____ me.
15. That isn't _____ what I _____.
16. With _____, that is not what I _____.

Rephrasing

17. Perhaps I haven't _____ myself _____. _____, what I'm _____ to say is . . .
18. _____, I'm probably not _____ myself _____. Let me _____ it _____ way . . .
19. Perhaps I should make that _____ by _____ . . .
20. _____ me to _____ that.
21. To be more _____, . . .
21. Put _____, . . .

Mini-Meeting 1

PART 1 Work in groups of 2. Think of two subjects you can talk about without having to think too much. When you've finished your first subject, change roles with your partner. Then change roles again until all four subjects are finished.

PART 2 Change partners but use the same subjects.

Reminder

In all these mini meetings you can use your **own** topics, or any of the topics suggested in any unit of the book. There are two or three topics in each unit for variety — but use **any** topic. The important thing is the *language of meetings*.

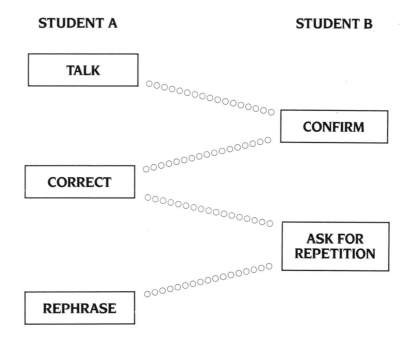

Nuclear Energy

Conventional sources running out
Alternative sources insufficient
Cheap and clean
Relatively safe

Enough coal and oil
Alternative sources renewable
Danger of accidents
Waste disposal

Marriage

Provides stability
Encourages responsibility
Most divorcees get remarried
Good for children

1 in 3 ends in divorce
Just financial contract
One partner not realistic
Not flexible enough

> If you're not confused you're not paying attention.

> I have suffered from being misunderstood, but I would have suffered a hell of a lot more if I had been understood.

> To deceive a diplomat speak the truth: he has no experience of it.

Mini-Meeting 2

Your teacher is going to choose a topic and tell you about it. As well as choosing a subject which will be both difficult and complicated, your teacher will speak at normal speed making no allowances for a non-native audience. You should ask for clarification whenever you don't understand.

Possible topics: Cricket
                    The Class System in England
                    The British or American Political System

PART 2 Choose a subject, perhaps something about your country which is not easily understood by foreigners, perhaps one of your hobbies or a sport. Think about your subject for a couple of minutes and then form groups of 2 and repeat the exercise.

PART 3 Work in groups of 2. Choose conflicting parts of the views below. As you give "your" views on the subject, your partner will interrupt to clarify what you are saying as much as possible. When you reply use the phrases in CORRECTING MISUNDERSTANDINGS and REPHRASING. When you've finished, change roles.

Traditional Family

Stability for children
'Normal'
Makes a stable society
Morally correct

Denies wife many possibilities
No mobility
Restricts development of individuals
Out-of-date

Match and Complete 1

bear	**something at (my)* fingertips**	_____
work	**something over**	_____
talk	**something in mind**	_____
have	**something our careful consideration**	_____
give	**something out**	_____

* Instead of my you may need his, her, your, etc.

1. Don't worry! We'll _____ something _____.

2. Why don't you _____ it _____ with the boss before you decide whether to resign or not?

3. Anyway, _____ what I said _____. There's still time to change your mind.

4. Well, thank you for explaining everything to us and we'll _____ it _____.

5. I'm afraid I don't _____ the facts _____. I'll have to get back to you on that this afternoon.

Match and Complete 2

a golden	**guess**	_____
a major	**contribution**	_____
a plenary	**opportunity**	_____
a viable	**session**	_____
a rough	**alternative**	_____

1. It was a _____; everybody was there.

2. What you suggest would be a _____ except for the fact that we have already invested heavily in the first project.

3. Getting that new contract will be a _____ to the success of our company in the years ahead.

4. We missed a _____ to buy shares in JCN when the dollar was low. It was a pity we couldn't raise enough cash.

5. At a _____ I'd say they're worth about 90,000 dollars.

Match and Complete 3

clarify	the meeting
solve	a comment
make	the problem
draw	the situation
hold	a conclusion

1. Where are we going to _____, in the small or large conference room?
2. Perhaps if I explained in more detail it would _____.
3. If I might _____ on that; I'll be very brief.
4. I'm not quite sure how we are going to _____ _____; it's very complex.
5. I think we have to _____ that they are not very interested in our proposal.

Match and Complete 4

Which prepositions go in the following expressions?

at   in   to   of

_____ **this juncture**

_____ **my knowledge**

_____ **lieu** _____

_____ **the long run**

_____ **the long term**

1. _____ it's better to buy the best machines. Even if they're more expensive, they last for years.
2. I think that, _____, we should consider selling out. However, for the moment, I agree that we should continue as we are.
3. _____ I would like to sum up what has been said.
4. We would be prepared to take a 10% holding _____ the sum due.
5. No registered letter has come today _____; but I'll check with the others.

Match and Complete 5

Which prepositions go in the following expressions?

from   **beside**   **at**   **of**

_____ **the moment**

_____ **note**

_____ **the outset**

_____ **the point**

_____ **this point**

1. I knew that this wasn't going to work _____, but nobody would listen to me.
2. The fact that you don't want to go is _____, you have no choice.
3. I'm sorry, Dr Jones is not here _____. Can I take a message?
4. I see nothing _____ in this paper: it's all been said before.
5. I think we should take a break _____.

"As you were saying, Primley, before Ferguson sneezed – we have here the ultimate micro-electronic breakthrough of the Eighties . . ."

Discussion

Communication

There are three big problems with communication. First, negotiators may not be talking to each other, or at least not in such a way as to be understood. Frequently each side has given up on the other and is no longer attempting any serious communication with it. Instead they talk merely to impress third parties or their own constituency. Rather than trying to dance with their negotiating partner toward a mutually agreeable outcome, they try to trip him up. Rather than trying to talk their partner into a more constructive step, they try to talk the spectators into taking sides. Effective communication between the parties is all but impossible if each plays to the gallery.

Even if you are talking directly and clearly to them, they may not be hearing you. This constitutes the second problem in communication. Note how often people don't seem to pay enough attention to what you say. Probably equally often, you would be unable to repeat what they said. In a negotiation, you may be so busy thinking about what you are going to say next, how you are going to respond to that last point or how you are going to frame your next argument, that you forget to listen to what the other side is saying now. Or you may be listening more attentively to your constituency than to the other side. Your constituents, after all, are the ones to whom you will have to account for the results of the negotiation. They are the ones you are trying to satisfy. It is not surprising that you should want to pay close attention to them. But if you are not hearing what the other side is saying, there is no communication.

The third communication problem is misunderstanding. What one says, the other may misinterpret. Even when negotiators are in the same room, communication from one to the other can seem like sending smoke signals in a high wind. Where the parties speak different languages the chance for misinterpretation is compounded. For example, in Persian, the word "compromise" apparently lacks the positive meaning it has in English of "a midway solution both sides can live with", but only has a negative meaning as in "her virtue was compromised" or "our integrity was compromised." Similarly, the word "mediator" in Persian suggest "meddler", someone who is barging in uninvited. In early 1980 U.N. Secretary General Waldheim flew to Iran to deal with the hostage question. His efforts were seriously set back when Iranian national radio and television broadcast in Persian a remark he reportedly made on his arrival in Tehran: "I have come as a *mediator* to work out a *compromise.*" Within an hour of the broadcast, his car was being stoned by angry Iranians.

From *Getting to Yes*, Fisher and Ury, Penguin Books.

How far do your agree with the above?
Can you think of any misinterpretations between English and your language?

7 Questioning

Language Awareness

How do you:

1. Ask a general question?

_____

Is your question acceptable in all situations?

2. Ask someone to give you more information about a subject?

_____

3. Give yourself time to think of an answer?

_____

4. Refuse to answer?

_____

Is your phrase diplomatic enough?

5. Give yourself time to think by asking a question?

_____

Asking General Questions

[1]Would you [2]mind . . . ?

I was wondering if you . . . ?

I wonder if you could . . . ?

May I ask . . .

[1]Would you mind if I asked . . . ?

Asking questions is an important technique in meetings as they cannot be challenged — statements can. These are all polite question forms; it is consequently difficult to avoid answering them.

1. Be careful here! A **positive** response to these questions is: *No. of course not* or *Not at all*. A **negative** response is: *Well, yes I do mind actually.*
2. Use the *. . .ing* form after *mind*: *Would you mind telling . . .*

Asking for Further Information

Could you be a [1]little more [2]precise?

I'm sorry, but could you explain in a [1]little more [3]detail?

Could you give us some [4]details about . . .?

Would you care to [5]elaborate on that?

Could you [6]expand on that?

1. Suggests that the speaker has almost given you all the details you wanted. Leaving it out would make the phrase more abrupt (see page 12).
2. Not used as a verb in English.
   ▷ specific.
   ▷ explicit.
3. No ''s'' at the end of *detail*.
4. Here, there is an ''s'' because this use refers to individual details.
5. Give more details.
6. Give more information.

Playing for Time

That's a very [1]interesting question.

[2]That's a difficult question to answer.

I'm [3]glad you asked that question.

You have raised an important point there.

[2]I'm sure you will appreciate how complicated this matter is.

These are standard phrases which give you a little more time to think of a reply.

1. ▷ complex.
2. This can be an excuse for an answer which is going to be far from clear.
3. Happy — which may be the opposite of what you are feeling!

Saying Nothing

[1]Well, it's rather difficult to say at [2]present.

[1]I'm afraid I don't have enough information at my disposal to answer that.

[3]I'm afraid I'm not in a position to comment on that just [2]yet.

[4]I think we can leave the problem of . . . . . aside for a moment, the real issue is . . .

[5]I don't think we have enough time at our disposal to consider all the [6]implications of this particular aspect of the problem.

All of these phrases are ways of avoiding giving an answer.

1. These mean that you don't know enough to give an answer.
2. Suggest you will be able to answer the question in the future, which makes your refusal to answer more acceptable.
3. This either means the same as note 1 above, or that you do not have permission to say.
4. Suggests you consider the question to be either irrelevant or insignificant.
5. Lack of time prevents you answering.
6. ▷ ramifications.

Questioning

[1]It depends what you mean by . . .

I'm not quite sure what you mean by that.

I'm afraid I don't quite follow . . .

[2]I don't think it's quite as simple as that . . .

These phrases again give you time to think of an answer.

1. This is a way of throwing the question back at the speaker who is then obliged to explain in more detail what he/she means.
2. This either gives you an opportunity to explain something which is more complicated than people think, or it allows you to complicate the issue so much that nobody understands it or you anymore.

Check Yourself

Here are the most important expressions. Fill in each blank with an appropriate word. It is best to do this orally without writing in your book as you may want to check yourself again later.

You can use this page as an *aide memoire* while taking part in the Mini-Meetings.

Asking general questions

1. _____ you mind . . . ?
2. I was _____ if you . . .
3. I _____ if you could . . . ?
4. _____ I ask . . . ?
5. Would you _____ if I _____ . . . ?

Asking for further information

6. Could you be a _____ more _____?
7. I'm sorry, but could you _____ in a _____ more _____ ?
8. _____ you give us some _____ about . . . ?
9. Would you _____ to _____ on that?
10. _____ you _____ on that?

Playing for time

11. That's a very _____ _____.
12. That's a _____ question to _____.
13. I'm _____ you asked that _____.
14. You have _____ an important _____ there.
15. I'm _____ you will _____ how complicated this matter is.

Saying nothing

16. _____, it's _____ difficult to say at _____.
17. I'm afraid I don't have _____ information _____ my _____ to answer that.
18. I'm afraid I'm _____ in a _____ to comment on that _____ yet.
19. I think we can _____ the problem of . . . . . . _____ for a moment, the _____ issue is . . .
20. I don't think we have enough time at our _____ to consider all the _____ of this particular _____ of the problem.

Questioning

21. It _____ what you _____ by . . .
22. I'm not _____ sure _____ you mean _____ that.
23. I'm afraid I don't _____ _____ . . .
24. I don't _____ it's _____ as _____ as that . . .

Mini-Meeting 1

PART 1 Work in groups of 2. Think of two subjects you can talk about without having to think too much. When you've finished your first subject, change roles with your partner. Then change roles again until all four subjects are finished.

PART 2 Change partners but use the same subjects.

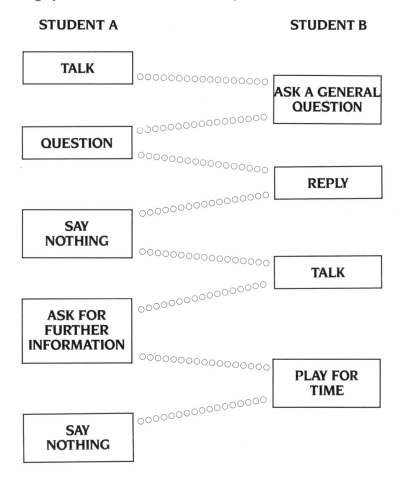

STUDENT A	STUDENT B
TALK	ASK A GENERAL QUESTION
QUESTION	REPLY
SAY NOTHING	TALK
ASK FOR FURTHER INFORMATION	PLAY FOR TIME
SAY NOTHING	

Classical Music

Moving
Relaxing
Great achievements
Like Shakespeare, helps us understand life

Pretentious
Socially elitist
Nobody can *like* Wagner!
Not *better* than jazz, just *different*

Big Cities

Cultural life
Shopping
More possibilities
Make economic sense

Dirty and polluted
Violence
Traffic and wasted time
Unnatural

Mini-Meeting 2

Work in groups of 2. There are two tables below: one for student A and one for student B. Do not look at your partner's table as the information missing from your table is in your partner's table. Each of you has information concerning six of the twelve projects A to L. You must obtain the information for the other six projects from your partner in order to complete your table. When your partner asks you for the information for which you only have a question mark, you should use one of the phrases from **Playing for Time Saying Nothing**, and **Questioning**. Take it in turns to ask the questions.

STUDENT A

PROJECT	COST (in Dollars)	FUNDING	LENGTH
A	10 billion	?	15 years
B			
C	?	National Governments	2½ years
D			
E	125,000	Voluntary	?
F			
G	?	World Bank	4 years
H			
I	3½ million	?	9 months
J			
K	90,000	International Monetary Fund	?
L			

STUDENT B

PROJECT	COST (in Dollars)	FUNDING	LENGTH
A			
B	?	World Bank	1½ years
C			
D	335,000	National Governments	?
E			
F	1½ million	?	5 years
G			
H	2 billion	International Monetary Fund	?
I			
J	200,000	?	13 years
K			
L	?	Voluntary	6 months

Match and Complete 1

jump	for time	_____
play	from scratch	_____
come	on the fence	_____
sit	to the point	_____
start	to conclusions	_____

1. We shouldn't _____ about this. Let's wait until we have a few more facts.

2. I wish he'd _____ — he's been talking non-stop for 20 minutes.

3. You never decide one way or the other — you just _____.

4. I think they're just _____. I don't believe that they have to check with head office at all.

5. When my first company went bankrupt, I had nothing — I had to _____ again.

Match and Complete 2

a blunt	question	_____
a pressing	asset	_____
a profitable	view	_____
a positive	problem	_____
a short-sighted	association	_____

1. So far we've had a _____ with JCN. If it continues like this we'll soon be able to retire!

2. The most _____ is the one concerning the rights of the staff.

3. We must be careful not to take a _____ of the problem; future generations are depending on us.

4. If I may ask a _____. How much do you want?

5. Jim's knowledge of computers will be a _____ to the firm.

Match and Complete 3

come	in the same boat	_____
beat	round in circles	_____
go	down to business	_____
be	to an agreement	_____
get	about the bush	_____

1. We _____, you know. We both risk losing our jobs.
2. Let's _____, shall we? We haven't got that much time left.
3. Let's not _____. How much do you want?
4. If we can _____ on the quantity, I'm sure the boss will be able to guarantee delivery.
5. We can't _____ all day. They say it's cheap; we say it's expensive. We're not making any progress at all.

Match and Complete 4

Which prepositions go in the following expressions?

in   under   at

_____ practice

_____ the present time

_____ pressure

_____ any price

_____ principle

1. _____ I agree with you, but there are still one or two details that we will need to discuss further.
2. He's _____ from the director to finalise the deal with Becket's.
3. We have to get that contract _____. It's a question of life or death for us.
4. I'm afraid we don't have any vacancies _____. We will, however, consider you for any future vacancies.
5. It looks good on paper, but it'll never work _____.

Match and Complete 5

Which prepositions go in the following expressions?

out   in   off   with   to   of

_____ **all probability**

_____ _____ **the question**

_____ **the record**

_____ **regard** _____

_____ **some respects**

1. It's _____. You can't go and that's final.

2. _____ I'll fail, but I think it's still worth a try.

3. What I told you yesterday was _____ and it is not to be repeated.

4. The plans are similar _____, but in others completely different.

5. _____ the proposed merger, I'd like to assure you that there will be no redundancies.

"Would you mind going around the corner, Mr Humphreys? That's the Chairman's space."

Discussion

UMS

Ums are sounds made in the nose that often seem to — um — punctuate English speech. They can express — um — different things:

hesitation,

disagreement,

embarrassment or

deliberation.

These sounds are neither meaningless nor unnecessary; nor are they the sign of an ineffective speaker. Look at these examples:

I think we could — um — live with that.

I'm — um — sure we can — um — come to some sort of — um — agreement.

This carries a very different meaning from:

I think we could live with that.

I'm sure we can come to some sort of agreement.

The first examples, said with a worried look, a hesitant forcing out of the words, show the speaker is not very sure and that he/she would like you to offer something more acceptable.

The second examples, said with a confident smile, and in a very relaxed way, imply that there are no serious problems, just a few details to clear up.

Obviously understanding **ums** will help in any negotiation with an Anglo-Saxon; using **ums** may help *you* to make your meaning clearer, and encourage acceptance of your conditions.

In addition, when you reply to a question, **ums** make it seem as if you had not foreseen the question, which in turn puts the person asking at ease. If you reply in a firm, direct way, it can appear premeditated and appear as a challenge, prompting the other party to go on the defensive. You may have wanted to show your decisiveness, but the result may be an attack! It's sometimes better to be — um — more hesitant, and less — um — dogmatic.

Does your language/culture use something similar to **ums?**

Can you think of any other ways of communicating the same thing?

8 Proposals

Language Awareness

How do you:

1. Propose something?

_____

Is your phrase strong, neutral or tentative?

2. Say you support a proposal?

_____

Is your phrase strong or weak?

3. Say you support a proposal but . . . ?

_____

4. Say you are against a proposal?

_____

Is your phrase strong or direct?

5. Say you are against a proposal but . . . ?

_____

Proposals, Recommendations and Suggestions — Strong

I strongly recommend that . . .

I suggest most strongly that . . .

I advise you most strongly to . . .

In our view, it is [1]high [2]time that . . .

In my view, the only [3]viable solution is . . .

1. Used for emphasis.
2. Use the past tense: *It's time we went.*
3. Realistic.

Proposals, Recommendations, and Suggestions — Neutral

I [1]propose that . . .

My [2]proposal is that . . .

1. ▷ recommend.
   ▷ suggest.
2. ▷ recommendation.
   ▷ suggestion.

Proposals, Recommendations and Suggestions — Tentative

I would [1]propose [2]that . . .

If I [2]may make a suggestion, we could . . .

I would like to put forward a proposal that . . .

I wonder if I might suggest . . .

Wouldn't it be a good idea to . . . ?

Wouldn't it be better to . . . ?

All of these use *would*, *could*, or *might*. They are all tentative which means that you do not commit yourself as much as when you use the phrases from neutral or strong proposals (see page 10).
1. ▷ recommend.
   ▷ suggest.
2. ▷ might — more formal.

Expressing Total Support

I am fully in favour of . . .

This proposal has my full support.

I can [1]thoroughly recommend that . . .

I should like to express my [2]total support for this . . .

I [3]totally agree with . . .

I entirely approve of . . .

Although these phrases express total support, they may be followed by a minor criticism. This criticism can be introduced by a phrase such as: "There is, however, just one thing . . .".
1. Completely.
2. ▷ wholehearted.
3. ▷ wholeheartedly.
   ▷ completely.
   ▷ entirely.

Expressing Support

I am in favour of . . .

I would certainly give my [1]backing to . . .

I would certainly [2]endorse such a proposal.

I [3]see no objection to that.

[4]I would not be opposed to that.

1. ▷ support.
2. ▷ approve of.
3. ▷ have.
4. Not a very enthusiastic way to express support!

Expressing Partial Support

My [1]initial reaction is favourable, but . . .

With certain [2]reservations, I would support your proposal.

I shouldn't like you to think that I'm necessarily against this in any way, but I can't help wondering . . .

1. First.
2. Conditions.

Expressing Total Opposition

I am [1]totally opposed to the proposal.

I see no [2]valid reason for supporting the proposal.

[3]Frankly, I think that's [4]out of the question.

[5]I'm afraid this proposal leaves a great deal to be desired.

1. ▷ completely.
   ▷ wholly.
   ▷ definitely.
2. Good/real.
3. Honestly — Used to introduce something which is almost certainly disagreeable.
4. Impossible.
5. This means that you don't think the proposal is good enough.

Expressing Opposition

I am opposed to the proposal.

I'm afraid I can't support the proposal.

[1]As it stands, I would not be able to give it my backing.

Without [2]substantial changes, I cannot give the proposal my support.

1. As it is. This implies that it should be changed.
2. Considerable/large.

Expressing Tentative Opposition

[1]On the face of it, this seems quite a good suggestion, but . . .

I can see [2]many problems in adopting this.

I'm not sure the proposal is [3]feasible.

This proposal is likely to present difficulties.

I'm not convinced that this proposal is really [4]worthwhile.

1. This implies that in-depth study of the proposal will show it is not as good as it looks.
2. ▷ certain.
   ▷ some.
3. Possible to do.
4. Worth the time or the effort.

Check Yourself

Here are the most important expressions. Fill in each blank with an appropriate word. It is best to do this orally without writing in your book as you may want to check yourself again later.

You can use this page as an *aide memoire* while taking part in the Mini-Meetings.

Strong proposals etc.

1. I _____ recommend that . . .
2. I _____ most _____ that . . .
3. In our _____, it is high _____ that . . .
4. _____ my view, the only _____ solution is . . .

Neutral proposals etc.

5. I _____ that . . .
6. My _____ is that . . .

Tentative proposals etc.

7. I _____ _____ that . . .
8. If I _____ make a _____, we could . . .
9. I would like to_____ _____ a proposal that . . .
10. I _____ if I _____ suggest . . .

Expressing total support

11. I am _____ in _____ of . . .
12. This _____ has my full _____.
13. I can thoroughly _____ that . . .

Expressing support

14. I am _____ _____ of . . .
15. I _____ certainly _____ my _____ to . . .
16. I would _____ endorse _____ a proposal.

Expressing partial support

17. My _____ reaction is _____, but . . .
18. With certain _____, I would _____ your proposal.

Expressing total opposition

19. I am _____ opposed _____ the proposal.
20. _____, I think that's _____ of the question.
21. I'm afraid this proposal leaves a _____ deal to be _____.

Expressing opposition

22. I'm afraid I _____ _____ the proposal.
23. As it _____, I _____ not be able to give it my _____.

Expressing tentative opposition

24. On the _____ of it, this seems _____ a good _____, but . . .
25. I can _____ many problems in _____ this.
26. I'm not _____ that this proposal is really _____.

Mini-Meeting 1

PART 1 Work in pairs. Think of two or three proposals you would like to make to improve the efficiency of your organisation or company. Make these proposals to your partner.

PART 2 Change partners and repeat the exercise.

> *If you wish to be a success in the world, promise everything, deliver nothing.*

> *A diplomat is somebody who can tell you to go to hell in such a way that you look forward to the trip.*

Mini-Meeting 2

Work in groups of 3. Student A choose one of the proposals below. You should propose the same thing 3 times, each time you should make it more acceptable to the group. When student A has finished his first proposal, change roles. Keep changing roles. Students B and C are reacting to student A's proposal not to each other.

Use the pattern for your discussion given on page 84.

Remember it is more important to practise the language of meetings than to worry too much about the content of your discussion.

1. To restrict smoking in public places
2. To maintain or reintroduce capital punishment
3. To introduce flexible working hours
4. To increase holidays from 4 weeks to 6 weeks a year
5. To allow citizens to choose whether to wear seat belts or not
6. To prohibit tobacco advertising
7. To ban violence on television
8. To reduce the speed limit on motorways to 80 kms/h
9. To maintain or reintroduce military service
10. To cancel all space exploration programmes

Pattern for Mini-meeting 2 on page 83.

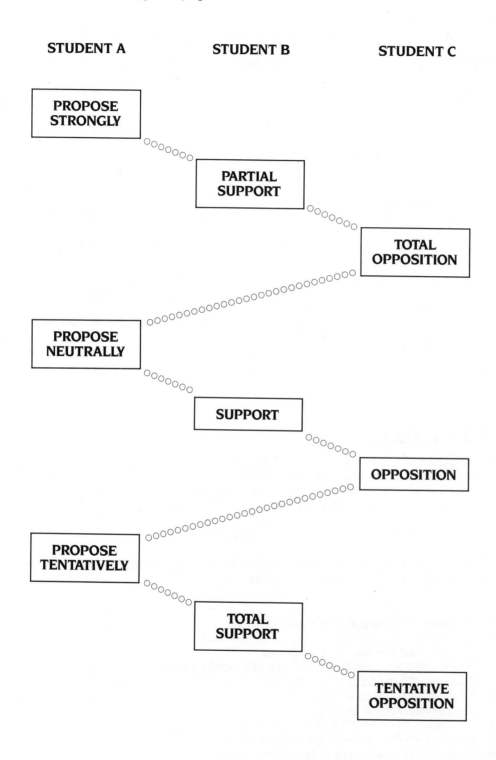

STUDENT A   STUDENT B   STUDENT C

PROPOSE STRONGLY

PARTIAL SUPPORT

TOTAL OPPOSITION

PROPOSE NEUTRALLY

SUPPORT

OPPOSITION

PROPOSE TENTATIVELY

TOTAL SUPPORT

TENTATIVE OPPOSITION

Match and Complete 1

reach   the subject   _____

submit   the difficulty   _____

chair   a proposal   _____

broach   a decision   _____

resolve   the meeting   _____

1. We have to _____ soon; the deadline's on Monday.
2. Perhaps we ought to _____ at tomorrow's meeting; we have to discuss it sometime.
3. Who's going to _____ this afternoon?
4. I'd like to _____ that smoking be banned in meetings.
5. We can _____ quite simply — we can dismiss him.

Match and Complete 2

a notable   investment   _____

a concrete   understanding _____

a frank   exception   _____

a mutual   proposal   _____

a long-term   discussion   _____

1. It was a _____, everybody put their cards on the table and said what they wanted to say quite openly.
2. The British don't like learning foreign languages, but Robert is a _____; he speaks 4 languages.
3. As _____ I can see its value, but I still think we need something which will bring us rewards in the near future.
4. We've been going round the problem for 30 minutes now, what we need is _____.
5. Well, we seem to have reached _____. We obviously have a firm basis on which to proceed.

Match and Complete 3

dodge   a choice   _____

adjourn   a threat   _____

pose   the meeting   _____

propose   the issue   _____

make   a solution   _____

1. Do you think they really _____ to us? They're so much smaller than us.
2. Sooner or later we have to _____, do we want to go ahead or not?
3. I'd like to _____ until tomorrow at 10.
4. It's no good trying to _____, we have to discuss it sometime.
5. Richard's going to _____ which should be accepted by the director.

Match and Complete 4

a bona fide   approach   _____

a bargaining   priority   _____

a heated   position   _____

a cost-conscious   discussion   _____

a high   proposal   _____

1. We had a _____ about the budget for next year; everybody was really shouting at each other.
2. I know you have your doubts about it, but I think they've made us a _____.
3. When deciding the allocations for the coming year, we should take a _____.
4. This is the most important item and it should be given a _____.
5. I don't think they'll accept it, but as a _____ I can see its value.

Match and Complete 5

Which prepositions go in the following expressions?

to   on   for   of   in

             _____ **this respect**

             _____ **response** _____

             _____ **return** _____

             _____ **the safe side**

             _____ **the sake** _____

1. _____ your support during the meeting, I'd be prepared to put forward your candidature for Head of Project.

2. _____ the company, you'll have to resign.

3. _____ I agree with you. I don't think the price of petrol will drop either.

4. To be _____ let's wait for confirmation before we telex Head Office.

5. What did they say _____ your offer?

"Wouldn't it be a good idea to replace the whole thing with a silicon chip?"

Discussion

The Proper Place of Tactics?

Consider two announcements made to passengers waiting on an aircraft for takeoff. The first 'We regret to have to inform you that because . . . and because . . . and because . . . there will be a delay of five minutes in our departure.' And the alternative: 'We are pleased to tell you that there will be no more than five minutes' delay in our departure, which is due to . . .'

In the first example, the passengers do not know what is going to follow the 'We regret to have to inform you . . .' It could mean a long delay, even having to change planes, etc. In the second case the minor delay is immediately announced as such. In doing anything there is rarely a neutral position: something is done in a good way or bad way. Tactics can be the art of doing something in the best way. But from whose point of view? Clearly from the point of view of the person operating the strategy, but this includes morals and also consideration for other parties.

The war of combat analogy can be taken too far. We can get into the habit of thinking only in terms of win-lose situations: 'I can only win if the other party loses.' Yet in many situations the purpose of negotiations or tactics is to ensure that all parties benefit: a win-win situation. In the example of the airline announcement the second version is better for all parties. A powerful general tactic is to align your interests with those of the other party so that both parties are working in roughly the same direction.

Nor should it be assumed that tactics only involve other parties. There may be tactics in building up a business or in doing a scientific experiment. Tactics refer to the implementation of the overall strategy — not just to beating an opponent.

A key element in tactics (or it may be part of strategy) is to provide a 'fallback' position. If things do not work out as desired where does that leave you? This may seem to be the opposite of risk-taking and commitment, but it is not. The better able you are to design your fallback, the better able you are to take a risk. There is a saying (attributed to Martina Navratilova among others) that in a plate of ham and eggs the hen is involved but the pig is committed. I am not convinced that that shows good sense on the part of the pig.

From *Tactics, the Art and Science of Success* by Edward de Bono, Fontana/Collins.

Do you agree with the author's view of tactics?
Why does the author consider that the pig is not showing good sense?

9 Persuading

IT WOULD BE IN YOUR OWN INTEREST TO...

Language Awareness

How do you:

1. Ask questions to persuade someone?

_____

Is your phrase acceptable in all situations?

2. Add information to make your argument more convincing?

_____

3. Say that someone's argument is not very sound?

_____

Is your phrase acceptable in all situations?

4. Say that you're not convinced?

_____

Is your phrase very direct?

5. Tell someone not to worry about something?

_____

Asking Questions

Have you taken into account . . . ?

Has it ¹occurred to you that . . . ?

Do you ²realise that . . . ?

I was wondering if you'd thought of . . . ?

³Wouldn't you agree that . . . ?

³Wouldn't it be a good idea to . . . ?

1. *Here* had the idea.
2. Understand.
3. Note the use of the negative (see page 11)

Adding Information

There are, ¹if I may say so, certain points you should bear in mind . . .

There are other considerations. For example, . . .

²If we look at it in another light . . .

²Seen from another angle, one could say . . .

I wonder if you've considered . . .

1. This is a way of making this phrase **more** polite; but is not impolite without the expression.
2. These mean that you are going to look at the problem in another way.

Challenging

I wonder if that view is ¹justified in the ²light of . . .

I don't think you ³fully ⁴appreciate the fact that . . .

It would be in your own interest to . . .

I would be inclined to . . ., if I were you.

This section is more direct than the previous two sections. You should be careful when using these phrases as they can cause offence.

1. Correct.
2. Could be followed by a phrase like: *the economic situation*.
3. Without *fully* this phrase would become a lot stronger.
4. *Here* understand.

Expressing Reservation

I have [1]certain [2]reservations about . . .

I think we should give ourselves time to [3]reflect on . . .

I'm rather [4]worried about . . .

[5]Under no circumstances [6]should we come to a [7]hasty decision on this.

I am afraid such a decision might lead to . . .

I feel that in view of . . . . . . it would be [8]prudent to . . .

I can't help feeling that . . .

1. ▷ serious — stronger.
2. Limiting conditions.
   ▷ misgivings — which means *doubts*.
3. ▷ think about
   ▷ consider.
4. ▷ sceptical — stronger.
5. ▷ in.
6. Inversion of subject and auxiliary after *under no circumstances*.
7. Made too quickly.
8. Sensible.

Reassuring

There's no [1]cause for concern as far as . . . . . . is concerned.

Let me [2]assure you straightaway on that point.

I can assure you that . . .

We understand your concern about . . . and we assure you that we will do everything in our power to . . .

We share your concern about this, and you may [3]rest assured that . . .

You need have no fears about . . .

1. Reason.
2. ▷ reassure.
3. Feel confident.

Check Yourself

Here are the most important expressions. Fill in each blank with an appropriate word. It is best to do this orally without writing in your book as you may want to check yourself again later.

You can use this page as an *aide memoire* while taking part in the Mini-Meetings.

Asking questions

1. _____ you _____ into account . . .
2. Has _____ occurred _____ you that . . .
3. Do you _____ that . . .
4. I was _____ if you'd _____ of . . . ?
5. Wouldn't you _____ that . . .
6. _____ it _____ a good idea to . . .

Adding information

7. There are, _____ I may _____ so, certain points you should _____ in mind . . .
8. _____ are other _____. For example, . . .
9. If we _____ at it in another _____ . . .
10. _____ from another _____, one _____ say . . .
11. I wonder _____ you've _____ . . .

Challenging

12. I _____ if that view is _____ in the _____ of . . .
13. I don't _____ you fully _____ the fact that . . .
14. It would be in _____ own _____ to . . .
15. I would be _____ to . . ., if I _____ you.

Expressing reservation

16. I have _____ _____ about . . .
17. I think we should _____ ourselves time to _____ on . . .
18. I'm rather _____ about . . .
19. _____ no circumstances _____ we come to a _____ decision on this.
20. I am _____ such a decision might _____ to . . .
21. I feel that in _____ of . . . it would be _____ to . . .
22. I can't _____ feeling that . . .

Reassuring

23. There's no _____ for _____ as far as . . . is concerned.
24. Let me _____ you _____ away _____ that point.
25. I can _____ you that . . .
26. We _____ your concern about . . . and we _____ you that we will _____ everything in our _____ to . . .
27. We _____ your concern about this, and you _____ rest _____ that . . .
28. You need _____ no _____ about . . .

Mini-Meeting 1

PART 1 Work in groups of 2. Think of two subjects about which you can try and persuade your partner. When you've finished your first subject, change roles with your partner. Keep changing roles until all four subjects are finished.

PART 2 Change partners but use the same subjects.

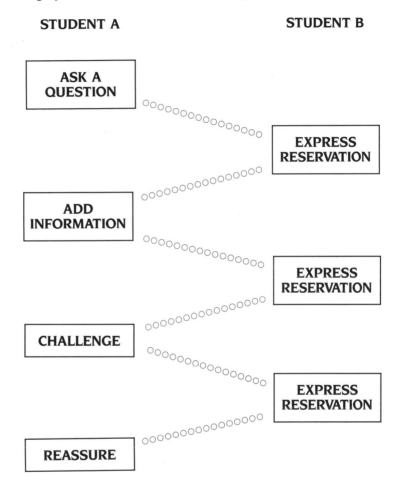

STUDENT A   STUDENT B

ASK A QUESTION

EXPRESS RESERVATION

ADD INFORMATION

EXPRESS RESERVATION

CHALLENGE

EXPRESS RESERVATION

REASSURE

Television

Keeps us informed	Violence
Education	Replaces hobbies
Helps the lonely	Kills conversation
Top quality entertainment	Affects children

> *We are more easily persuaded, in general, by the reasons we ourselves discover, than by those which have been suggested to us by others.*

> *The secret of success in life consists in knowing how to change men's minds.*

> *Negotiation is a process in which both sides win.*

Mini-Meeting 2

PART 1 Work in groups of 2. You and your partner are thinking of going on holiday. Unfortunately, you do not see things in the same way. Using the list below, try and persuade your partner to change his/her mind.

PART 2 Now change partners and roles.

STUDENT A	STUDENT B
overcrowded	not in September
sea polluted	not in the little village I've found
noisy discos	only two discos and both close early
hotel expensive	it's a small, family hotel
too far away from sights	we can hire a car
hiring too expensive	I checked, small cars are cheap
not hot enough	average temperature of 30 degrees
not safe at night	as safe as here
cost too much	no more than last year
taking the dogs	be no trouble

Match and Complete 1

reach	a question	_____
drive	a stalemate	_____
keep	a solution	_____
study	an open mind	_____
find	a hard bargain	_____

1. You _____, but I'll take it.
2. If you _____ long enough, you can usually find an answer.
3. We'll soon_____; they won't give any more and neither will we.
4. If we don't _____ soon, we'll have to abandon the project.
5. You should _____ during the negotiations; be flexible.

Match and Complete 2

an open	outcome	_____
a constructive	block	_____
a stumbling	mind	_____
a successful	disadvantage	_____
a major	attitude	_____

1. The only _____ to getting their agreement might be the proposed length of the project.
2. I can see at least one _____ in adopting this approach — the long-term effects.
3. You should keep _____ when negotiating; you have to be flexible to be a good negotiator.
4. We appreciate the_____ you've taken on this issue.
5. We hope that these talks will have _____ _____.

Match and Complete 3

think   something aside   _____

make   something out of hand   _____

leave   something over   _____

dismiss something into account   _____

take   something clear   _____

1. I wouldn't _____ his offer _____ if I were you. Think about it before you say no.

2. Let me _____ it _____ that I will not tolerate staff being late.

3. Let's _____ the problem of finance _____ for the moment. Have we found a suitable site?

4. Well, I'll _____ it _____, but I can tell you now that I'm not very enthusiastic.

5. If we _____ your expenses _____, you will see that we're not making money but losing it.

Match and Complete 4

lose   headway   _____

show   goodwill   _____

make   common ground   _____

take   face   _____

find   action   _____

1. Why can't we _____ any _____ in these negotiations? There's been no progress at all.

2. To _____ we are prepared to reduce the price by 5%.

3. We'll have to _____ soon — the deadline is Friday.

4. Do you think we'll _____ if we simply admit we made a mistake?

5. Well, I think we've _____ some _____ and I'm sure we'll now be able to find a compromise.

Match and Complete 5

Which prepositions go in the following expressions?

in   at   on   behind   ahead of

_____ the short term

_____ schedule

_____ schedule

_____ schedule

_____ short notice

1. We're exactly _____: everything should be finished when we said it would be.

2. If we get any further _____, we'll have to ask the bank for another loan.

3. Well, for the first time ever we are _____. We'll be finished well before the end of the month.

4. I don't know if I'll be able to get that much money together _____ _____. You should have given me more time.

5. _____ it's going to cost a lot, but after a couple of years we should be making a lot of money.

"Six thousand a year may not sound much, but look at it this way."

Discussion

Negotiators are people first

A basic fact about negotiation, easy to forget in corporate and international transactions, is that you are dealing not with abstract representatives of the "other side," but with human beings. They have emotions, deeply held values, and different backgrounds and viewpoints, and they are unpredictable. So are you.

This human aspect of negotiation can be either helpful or disastrous. The process of working out an agreement may produce a psychological commitment to a mutually satisfactory outcome. A working relationship where trust, understanding, respect, and friendship are built up over time can make each new negotiation smoother and more efficient. And people's desire to feel good about themselves, and their concern for what others will think of them, can often make them more sensitive to another negotiator's interests.

On the other hand, people get angry, depressed, fearful, hostile, frustrated, and offended. They have egos that are easily threatened. They see the world from their own personal vantage point, and they frequently confuse their perceptions with reality. Routinely, they fail to interpret what you say in the way you intend and do not mean what you understand them to say. Misunderstanding can reinforce prejudice and lead to reactions that produce counter-reactions in a vicious circle; rational exploration of possible solutions becomes impossible and a negotiation fails. The purpose of the game becomes scoring points, confirming negative impressions, and apportioning blame at the expense of the substantive interests of both parties.

Failing to deal with others sensitively as human beings prone to human reactions can be disastrous for a negotiation. Whatever else you are doing at any point during a negotiation, from preparation to follow-up, it is worth asking yourself, "Am I paying enough attention to the people problem?"

From Getting to Yes, Fisher and Ury, Penguin Books.

Do you agree with the above?
Could this be said of negotiating in your country?

10 Importance and Certainty

Language Awareness

How do you:

1. Say something is important?

_____

Is your phrase very strong?

2. Tell someone that something is not very important?

_____

3. Say something is certain?

_____

4. Say something is probable?

_____

5. Say something is possible?

_____

6. Say something is improbable?

_____

7. Say something is uncertain?

_____

Degrees of Importance

Emphatic Views

I particularly want to ¹emphasize the fact that . . .
It is ²essential to realise that . . .
This issue is highly significant.
I feel this is a ³vital issue.
I consider this point of the ⁴utmost importance.

1. ▷ highlight.
   ▷ underline.
   ▷ stress.
2. ▷ imperative.
3. Very important.
   ▷ crucial.
4. ▷ greatest.

Neutral Views

I ¹attach considerable importance to . . .
Allow me to emphasize at this ²juncture that . . .
We mustn't ³underestimate the importance of . . .
It is well worth noting that . . .
⁴We cannot stress too much the importance of . . .
Let me say again how much importance I attach to . . .

1. Give
2. ▷ point
   ▷ stage
3. Give something less value than it deserves.
4. The idea is "because it is so important".

Tentative Views

I would like to remind you that . . .
I wish to draw your attention to . . .
We ¹cannot ²overlook the fact that . . .
I believe this ³warrants further discussion.

1. ▷ mustn't.
2. ▷ ignore.
3. Is worth.
   ▷ calls for

Playing Down a Point

These are minor issues when one considers . . .
But this is only of secondary importance.
But this is, ¹after all, a relatively small point.
I'm afraid I ²regard that as of relatively minor significance.
I'm afraid I'm not totally convinced of the importance of . . .

1. Nevertheless.
2. See.

Degrees of Certainty

Certain

I'm [1]certain that . . .
It's [2]certain that . . .
There's no [3]doubt that . . .
Without [3]doubt, . . .
Undoubtedly, . . .

1. ▷ sure.
   ▷ convinced.
2. ▷ obvious.
   sure cannot be used in this position.
3. ▷ question.

Probable

I'm [1]almost certain that . . .
It's [2]highly probable that . . .
It's quite [3]likely that . . .

1. ▷ virtually - more certain.
2. ▷ very.
3. ▷ probable.

Possible

This [1]could well . . .
It's possible that . . .
It's not out of the question that . . .
It's not impossible that . . .
I think there is [2]every possibility that . . ..

1. ▷ might — more possible.
   ▷ may — most possible.
   Here very little difference between them.
2. *Here* all/complete.

Unlikely

It is [1]highly improbable that . . .
It is [2]highly unlikely that . . .
There's very little [3]likelihood of . . .

1. ▷ most.
2. ▷ extremely.
   ▷ very.
   ▷ most.
3. Probability.

Uncertain

I'm not [1]certain that . . .
I have doubts about . . .
I doubt [2]if . . .
There is some doubt as to whether this . . .
I'm uncertain about . . .

1. ▷ sure.
   ▷ convinced.
2. ▷ whether.

Check Yourself

Here are the most important expressions. Fill in each blank with an appropriate word. It is best to do this orally without writing in your book as you may want to check yourself again later.

You can use this page as an *aide memoire* while taking part in the Mini-Meetings.

Emphatic views

1. I _____ want to _____ the fact that . . .
2. It is _____ to realise that . . .
3. This _____ is highly _____.
4. I _____ this is a _____ issue.
5. I _____ this point of the _____ importance

Neutral views

6. I _____ considerable _____ to . . .
7. _____ me to _____ at this juncture that . . .
8. We _____ _____ the importance of . . .
9 It is _____ worth _____ that . . .

Tentative views

10. I would like to _____ you that . . .
11. We cannot _____ the _____ that . . .
12. I believe this _____ further _____.

Playing down a point

13. _____ are _____ issues when one considers . . .
14. But this is only of _____ _____ . . .
15. But this is, after _____, a _____ small _____.

Certain

16. I'm _____ that . . .
17. There's no _____ that . . .

Probable

18. I'm _____ certain that . . .
19. It's _____ probable that . . .

Possible

20. This _____ well . . .
21. It's not _____ of the _____ that . . .

Unlikely

22. It is _____ _____ that . . .
23. There's very _____ _____ of . . .

Uncertain

24. I'm not _____ that . . .
25. I _____ doubts _____ . . .
26. There is some _____ as to _____ this . . .

Mini-Meeting 1

PART 1 Work in groups of 2. Think of two subjects you can talk about without having to think too much. When you've finished your first subject, change roles with your partner.

PART 2 Change partners but use the same subjects.

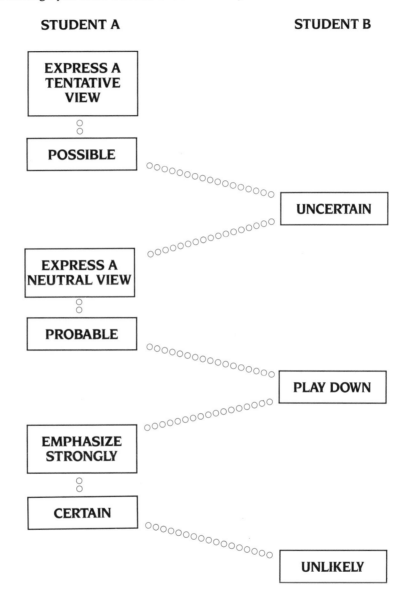

STUDENT A   STUDENT B

EXPRESS A TENTATIVE VIEW

POSSIBLE

UNCERTAIN

EXPRESS A NEUTRAL VIEW

PROBABLE

PLAY DOWN

EMPHASIZE STRONGLY

CERTAIN

UNLIKELY

Possible topics

Public transport
Private education
Censorship of the Press
Best system of management

> I wish I could be half as sure
> of anything as some people
> are of everything.

> I am not young enough to
> know everything.

Mini-Meeting 2

Work in groups of 2. Using the list of predictions below, tell each other how certain or uncertain you think they are. You should also justify your answer. Student A should say how certain he/she is about number 1; student B should reply saying how much importance she/he gives to such a prediction. Then student B should decide about number 2

1. There will be no more nuclear power stations built.
2. England will win the next World Cup.
3. Cars will be obsolete by the year 2200.
4. The United Nations will no longer exist by the year 2000.
5. Life expectancy will continue to rise.
6. People will be able to shop by computer.
7. People will be able to go to the moon for a holiday.
8. Unemployment will cease to exist.
9. Soon over 50% of the world's population will be over 65.
10. All factories will be fully automated.
11. Europe will become one country with one parliament.
12. Smoking will be illegal.
13. English will become the world language.
14. A world government will be established.
15. The world will blow itself up before the year 2025.
16. A cure for cancer will be found.
17. Marriage will be a thing of the past.
18. Computers will put most of us out of work.
19. Family size will be restricted by law.
20. Learning a foreign language will only take a week.

Match and Complete 1

call   a concession _____

make   the fact that _____

pave   an objection _____

raise   an adjournment _____

overlook the way   _____

1. If we _____ on the dates, they **might** be ready to reduce their commission.
2. As it's nearly midday, I'd like to _____ until after lunch.
3. Don't _____ he is the manager's brother-in-law.
4. I do hope that my offer will _____ to a full settlement.
5. If we _____ to the scheme the boss won't be at all pleased.

Match and Complete 2

a feasible project _____

a positive resort _____

a crucial attitude _____

a last   agreement _____

a tentative issue   _____

1. Everybody had a _____ so we got everything done in record time.
2. We managed to reach a _____, but we didn't finalise anything.
3. From what you've shown us, it seems to be a _____ and it should work.
4. I would only consider walking out of the negotiations as a _____. But I agree we should do it if everything else fails.
5. I feel this is a _____ and one which should be dealt with in detail.

Match and Complete 3

opening   trust   _____

common   consequences _____

protracted   ground   _____

grave   negotiations   _____

mutual   remarks   _____

1. It seems to me that we've found some _____
_____ here as we both agree that the project should be speeded up.
2. May I emphasise that such a decision may have _____
_____ for the future of the firm.
3. I'm glad that at last these _____ are finished.
4. Without _____ we won't get anywhere;
we have to trust each other.
5. The Chairman's _____ were, as usual, far too long.

Match and Complete 4

Which prepositions go in the following expressions?

on   at   in   from

_____ sight

_____ the spot

_____ this stage

_____ stake

_____ the start

1. Someone will have to go there as we haven't got a representative _____
_____.
2. I can't believe it — after 2 years the end is _____.
3. Be careful, there's a lot _____; we risk losing a big customer.
4. I think we can afford to be generous _____.
5. I knew there was something wrong _____. I told you so
before we signed the contract.

Match and Complete 5

Which prepositions go in the following expressions?

in   for   on   of

_____ **this subject**

_____ **the surface**

_____ **theory**

_____ **the time being**

_____ **view** _____

1. I think we should continue _____, but look at the problem again in 2 months.

2. _____ your years of service, we're prepared to give you another chance. But don't do it again.

3. Have you got anything to say _____?

4. _____ this looks like a good idea, but if we look in a little more detail we can see that it is not feasible.

5. _____ it works, but we'll have to try it out before we can be sure.

"No, J. R., you were supposed to bring the management efficiency study."

Discussion

Look at the following list in groups of 3 or 4 and decide which would annoy or irritate you.
Which ones, if any, are you personally guilty of?
Can you think of any others?

Other People's Mannerisms

1. Banging the table to emphasise important points.
2. Leaning back in your chair.
3. Drumming your fingers or a pencil on the table.
4. Biting your nails.
5. Biting your lips.
6. Chewing gum.
7. Eating sweets.
8. Smoking.
9. Cleaning your fingernails.
10. Tapping your foot on the floor.
11. Doodling on a piece of paper.
12. Staring into space while talking.
13. Rattling keys or money in your pocket.
14. Keeping your hands in your pockets.
15. Twisting a ring on your finger.
16. Supporting your head on your hand.
17. Wetting your lips with your tongue.
18. Scratching your head.
19. Adjusting spectacles.
20. Thinking you're the only one in the room with **no** mannerisms at all!

11 Compromising

Language Awareness

How do you:

1. Offer a compromise to someone?

_____

Is your phrase tentative?

2. Ask if a compromise is acceptable?

_____

Is your phrase tentative?

3. Accept a compromise but add a condition?

_____

4. Reject a compromise but leave a chance for another compromise?

_____

5. Accept a compromise?

_____

6. Reject a compromise?

_____

Is your phrase very direct?

Offering a Compromise

We are prepared to . . ., on condition that . . .

I think we could . . ., [1]provided that . . .

We are ready to . . ., on the understanding that . . .

We are willing to . . ., with the proviso that . . .

We are [2]more than ready to . . ., as long as . . .

I believe we can . . ., if . . .

Any of the phrases in the first half may be used with any of the phrases in the second half.

a. If the condition is put first, the offer becomes slightly less positive.

b. If *would* is used, the offer becomes more tentative (see page 10).

c. If a past tense is used, the offer becomes even more tentative:

We would be prepared to . . . . ., on condition that you gave us 2 more weeks.

To ask if a compromise is acceptable, use:

Would you be prepared to . . . . ., on condition that . . .?

Are you prepared to . . . . ., on condition that . . .?

1. ▷ providing.
2. Used here for emphasis.

Asking if it's Acceptable

Is that acceptable?

[1]Would that be acceptable?

[1]Would that be satisfactory?

Is that acceptable as a compromise solution?

We hope that this will be acceptable.

1. Note the tentative use of *would* (see page 10).

Adding a Condition Positively

We see no objection [1]whatsoever, provided that . . .

[2]If we agreed, it would be conditional on . . .

Our agreement [3]is conditional on . . .

[2]If we agreed, we hope you would [4]reciprocate by . . .

If you would be [5]prepared to . . . . ., then we could . . .

1. Emphatic form of *whatever* which means *of any sort*.
2. ▷ if we agree, it would be conditional on . . .
   ▷ If we agree, it will be conditional on . . .
   The use of a past tense after *if* makes it more tentative. The use of *would* in the second part also makes it more tentative. There are therefore 3 possibilities.
3. ▷ would be.
4. Give in return.
5. ▷ willing.

Adding a Condition Negatively

We'd be [1]rather [2]reluctant to . . ., [3]unless . . .

I don't think we could . . ., unless . . .

We wouldn't be prepared to . . ., unless . . .

We have certain reservations about . . ., and [4]unless . . .

[5]Only if you . . ., would we be prepared to . . .

1. This softens the phrase. Stress *reluctant* not *rather* (see page 15).
2. Means you are not ready to do something.
3. Can be followed by a present tense or a past tense. The past tense is more tentative.
4. The condition first sounds more threatening or aggressive.
5. Note that the subject and auxillary verb of the second clause are inverted. *Only if* is totally different from, *If only* which means I *wish*: *If only I'd brought my camera.*

Accepting a Compromise

I think that would be [1]perfectly acceptable.

We see no objection to that.

That seems to be a [2]reasonable compromise.

[3]In a spirit of compromise, we would be willing to accept your offer.

To meet you halfway on this, I think we could agree to your condition.

1. Completely.
2. Neither more nor less than what is acceptable.
3. So that we can reach a compromise.

Rejecting a Compromise

We are not entirely convinced that this is a [1]viable solution to the problem.

Although we want to avoid a [2]deadlock as much as you do, we find your offer unacceptable.

[3]You leave us with little alternative but to . . .

In that case, we should very reluctantly have to . . .

In which case, we would be [4]virtually obliged to . . .

You put us in a difficult position.

1. *Here* possible.
2. A complete failure to reach agreement.
3. This means you have no choice.
4. Similar to *almost*.

Check Yourself

Here are the most important expressions. Fill in each blank with an appropriate word. It is best to do this orally without writing in your book as you may want to check yourself again later.

You can use this page as an *aide memoire* while taking part in the Mini-Meetings.

Offering a compromise

1. We are _____ to . . ., on _____ that . . .
2. I think we _____ . . ., _____ that . . .
3. We are _____ to . . ., on the _____ that . . .
4. We are _____ to . . ., with the _____ that . . .
5. We are _____ than _____ to . . ., _____ long as . . .
6. I _____ we can . . ., if . . .

Asking if it's acceptable

7. Is that _____?
8. _____ that be _____?
9. Would that be _____?
10 Is that _____ as a _____ solution?
11. We _____ that this will be _____.

Adding a condition positively

12. We see no _____ _____, provided that . . .
13. If we _____, it would be _____ on . . .
14. Our _____ is _____ on . . .
15. If we agreed, we _____ you would _____ by . . .
16. If you would be _____ to . . ., then we could . . .

Adding a condition negatively

17. We'd be _____ _____ to . . ., unless . . .
18. I don't think we _____ . . ., _____ . . .
19. We wouldn't be _____ to . . ., unless . . .
20. We _____ certain _____ about . . ., and unless . . .

Accepting a compromise

21. I think that would be _____ _____.
22. We _____ no _____ to that.
23. That seems to be a _____ _____.

Rejecting a compromise

24. We are not entirely _____ that this is a _____ solution _____ the problem.
25. Although we want to _____ a _____ as much as you do, we _____ your offer _____.
26. You _____ us with _____ alternative _____ to . . .
27. In that _____, we should very _____ have to . . .
28. In _____ case, we would be _____ obliged to . . .
29. You _____ us in a _____ position.

Mini-Meeting 1

PART 1 Work in groups of 2. Think of a subject you can use to practise compromising. When you've finished change roles with your partner and choose a new subject.

PART 2 Change partners. Use the same subjects, or choose new ones.

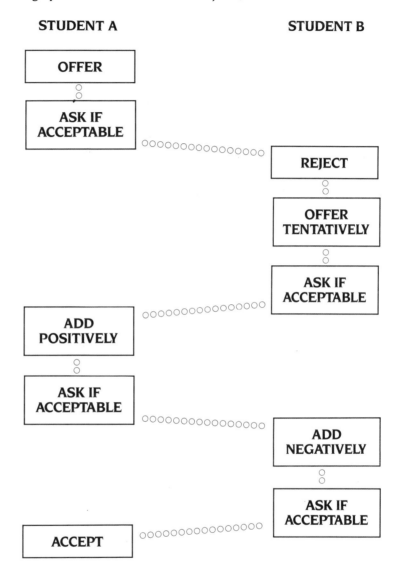

STUDENT A

STUDENT B

OFFER

ASK IF ACCEPTABLE

REJECT

OFFER TENTATIVELY

ASK IF ACCEPTABLE

ADD POSITIVELY

ASK IF ACCEPTABLE

ADD NEGATIVELY

ASK IF ACCEPTABLE

ACCEPT

Possible subjects

Selling your car to a colleague
Negotiating a salary
Buying a house

Negotiating your children's disco with the neighbours
Choosing viewing channels for the evening's TV

Mini-Meeting 2

Work in groups of 2. One of you will represent the unions while the other will be the representative from the management. Each of you has a list of 5 items you want from the other side and another list of 10 items which you are prepared to accept. Your partner can either accept or reject your offer, or add a condition. If your partner adds a condition, you can either accept or reject it, or add another condition. Each time you reach agreement cross off the items on your list.

MANAGEMENT

YOU WANT	PREPARED TO ACCEPT
1. Increased efficiency	1. Increase in salary
2. Reduction in sick leave	2. Flexitime
3. Shorter tea breaks	3. More training courses
4. Shorter lunch breaks	4. Better retirement plan
5. Increase in production	5. More sports facilities
6. Less time-wasting	
7. Willingness to work overtime when needed	
8. 10% reduction in the workforce	
9. No personal telephone calls	
10. No strikes	

Draw a line between the two columns when a compromise is reached.

UNIONS

YOU WANT	PREPARED TO ACCEPT
1. Increase in salary	1. Increased efficiency
2. Longer holidays	2. Shorter tea breaks
3. Flexitime	3. Less time-wasting
4. Better catering facilities	4. Willingness to work overtime when needed
5. More training courses	5. No personal telephone calls
6. Better retirement plan	
7. No redundancies without consultation	
8. A special club	
9. A bonus scheme linked to productivity	
10. More sports facilities	

Draw a line between the two columns when a compromise is reached.

Match and Complete 1

illustrate   a study   _____

clinch   a compromise   _____

undertake   the deal   _____

have   the point   _____

reach   a discussion   _____

1. To _____, I've brought along some interesting statistics.
2. We will have to _____ of the project before we can be sure of its potential.
3. Can we _____ on this tomorrow?
4. Did you manage to _____ with that difficult client?
5. I think we've _____ which is acceptable to us both.

Match and Complete 2

a fruitful   risk   _____

a compromise   outlook   _____

a positive   programme   _____

an on-going   solution   _____

a serious   collaboration   _____

1. We're taking _____; I hope we don't live to regret it.
2. Thank you for your co-operation and we look forward to _____ _____ in the future.
3. We appreciate the _____ you've shown and this has helped us enormously in our task.
4. What we need is _____ where both of us walk away from the table with something in our hands.
5. There is _____ covering this problem. It started two years ago and will probably continue for another two.

Match and Complete 3

avert	**a compromise**	_____
offer	**a crisis**	_____
close	**the floor**	_____
tackle	**the meeting**	_____
give	**the problem**	_____

1. If they don't _____, the negotiations will go on for ever.
2. Before I _____, may I thank everybody for coming.
3. I'd like to _____ to Miss Baker who has something to say about the financial side of things.
4. How are we going to _____? Perhaps you should study it first and then we'll all get together to listen to your suggestions.
5. With the price of oil increasing I don't see how we can _____.

Match and Complete 4

draw	**(your) comments on . . .**	_____
invite	**(your) position**	_____
meet	**(your) attention to . . .**	_____
understand	**(you) in the picture**	_____
put	**(you) halfway**	_____

1. I'd like to _____ paragraph 4 where it is stated quite clearly that . . .
2. To _____ on this, we could offer 5,000.
3. Of course we _____; however, we find it impossible to accept your offer.
4. Let me _____, the information we have suggests that . . .
5. At this point I'd like to _____ the overseas market.

Match and Complete 5

Which prepositions go in the following expressions?

by   with   to   in   of   on

_____ **the verge** _____

_____ **a view** _____

_____ **the way**

_____ **the whole**

_____ **a word**

_____ **writing**

1. I called you together today _____ offering you my resignation.
2. Oh, _____, I noticed there was a letter for you at the reception.
3. _____, I would agree with you. There are, however, one or two points . . .
4. We are _____ disaster. If we don't do something now, we're finished.
5. I'm not celebrating until I see it _____.
6. _____, I'm afraid the answer is 'No'.

"Aha! Trying to buy us off with huge salaries and great working conditions, huh?"

Discussion

The table below shows three ways of negotiating: **soft**, **hard** and **principled.**
Which of the three do you think is the most common in your country?
Which of the three do you think is the most effective?

PROBLEM Positional Bargaining: Which Game Should You Play?		SOLUTION Change the Game — Negotiate on the Merits
SOFT Participants are friends.	**HARD** Participants are adversaries.	**PRINCIPLED** Participants are problem-solvers.
The goal is agreement.	The goal is victory.	The goal is a wise outcome reached efficiently and amicably.
Make concessions to cultivate the relationship.	Demand concessions as a condition of the relationship.	**Separate the people from the problem.**
Be soft on the people and the problem.	Be hard on the problem and the people.	Be soft on the people, hard on the problem.
Trust others.	Distrust others.	Proceed independent of trust.
Change your position easily.	Dig in to your position.	**Focus on interests, not positions.**
Make offers.	Make threats.	Explore interests.
Disclose your bottom line.	Mislead as to your bottom line.	Avoid having a bottom line.
Accept one-sided losses to reach agreement.	Demand one-sided gains as the price of agreement.	**Invent options for mutual gain.**
Search for the single answer: the one *they* will accept.	Search for the single answer: the one *you* will accept.	Develop multiple options to choose from; decide later.
Insist on agreement.	Insist on your position.	Insist on using objective criteria.
Try to avoid a contest of will.	Try to win a contest of will.	Try to reach a result based on standards independent of will.
Yield to pressure.	Apply pressure.	Reason and be open to reasons; yield to principle, not pressure.

From *Getting to Yes*, Fisher and Ury, Penguin Books

12 Procedure for a formal meeting

This unit is different from the others in this book. It is concerned with meetings or conferences directed by a chairman/chairwoman. Much of the language used to control the meeting is very stylised so that the identical words are used on all occasions. The language presented here is subdivided into **more** and **less** formal. The phrase or phrases in each section before the space are **more formal**, those after it are **less formal.** Even so, because this language is used only in meetings which are controlled from the chair, it is all, by normal standards, formal.

Much of the language presented below is for the exclusive use of the person controlling the meeting from the chair.

One important introductory point must be made. In recent years, there has been much discussion of the language appropriate to addressing the person in the chair. For many years, *Chairman* was standard, and if the person in the chair was a woman, *Madam Chairman* was used. Some people found this last phrase ridiculous, and preferred *Chairwoman*.

In recent years the situation has become more complicated. Now, all of the following are used:

chairman, chairperson, chair, chairwoman

All except the last may be applied to either a man or a woman, while the last is used only if the person is known to be female.

To **address** the person in the chair the following will all be found:

Mr. Chairman, may I make a point here?
With **the Chairman's** permission, . . .
With **the Chair's** permission . . .

The first is used only if the person is male; the other two may be used to anyone. *Madam Chairman* now seems old fashioned. In *Who Cares about English Usage* (Penguin Books 1984) David Crystal says, among other things, the following:

> *Chairman* is one of the words which has caused most fuss, along with a few others ending in *-man.* . . . *Chairman* attracted special criticism, presumably because of a distinctive and influential social role involved in taking the chair at a meeting.
> Some people suggested *chairwoman* as a parallel to *chairman* — but it didn't catch on.
> The word which, in the end, came to be most widely used, especially in the USA, was *chairperson.* It's nowadays very widely used in publicity for academic conferences and the like . . . On the other hand the association of the new word with the extreme views of some feminists makes it a source of humour to some people. It still has only limited standing in the world of industry and commerce, where male domination evidently continues to be the norm.

Probably the best and most courteous course of action, is to ask anyone who is in the chair how they wish to be addressed, and what term they wish to use to describe their own function. In the examples below, *Chairman* is used, but the other alternatives discussed above can be substituted.

Opening

¹Ladies and Gentlemen, I declare the meeting open.

¹Right, shall we get started?
¹Let's get down to business, shall we?

1. See note above for formality levels.

The Minutes

¹May I read the minutes?
²Would someone move that the minutes of the last meeting be accepted?

³Has everyone seen the minutes?
³Can we take the minutes as read?

The minutes are a summary of what was said and done at the previous meeting.

1. If the minutes have not been circulated before the meeting, they are read out to check that they are an accurate summary of the previous meeting.
2. Someone should then say "I so move" and the minutes are accepted.
3. These mean that the minutes were circulated before the meeting. Anything which requires further discussion comes under *Matters Arising* on the agenda.

The Agenda

Has everyone received a copy of the agenda?
The first item on the agenda today is . . .
I would like to add an item to the agenda.
¹Could we delete item 5 from the agenda?

1. This means that either the problem has been resolved, or that the item is no longer relevant or important.

The Subject

The purpose of today's meeting is . . .
The first problem we have to consider is . . .
Perhaps we should first look at . . .

Giving the Floor

I'd like to ¹give the floor to ²Miss Hinton.

Mrs Williams, would you like to say something about this?

Mr Brown, I think you know something about this problem.

Have *you* got anything to say, John?
What are *your* views on this, Anne?

1. Give permission to speak.
2. The use of surnames or first names depends on the level of formality of the meeting; this is decided by the chairman/chairwoman.

Taking the Floor

Excuse me Mr Chairman, may I say something please?

With the Chair's permission, I'd like to [1]take up the point about . . .

1. This means that the point was mentioned among others and that you don't want to comment on all the points but just this one.

Could I just make a point about . . .?

Could I say something here, please?

Finishing a Point

Has anyone anything further [1]they wish to add before we move on to the next item on the agenda?

1. Note the use of a plural pronoun here. This is to avoid using the pronoun "he" which may offend the female participants.

Has anyone anything further to add?

Directing

[1]We seem to be losing sight of the main point. The question is . . .

This isn't really relevant to our discussion. What we're trying to do is . . .

Could you [2]stick to the subject, please?

Let's not get [3]sidetracked. The issue under discussion is . . .

These phrases are used when the discussion starts to wander and become irrelevant.
1. You are moving too far away from the subject.
2. Stay on and not move away from.
3. Keep to the main line of discussion, not digress.

Keeping Order

We can't all speak at once; Mr Newby, would you like to speak first?

[1]Mrs Wilson, would you mind addressing your remarks to the Chair, please.

[2]I shall have to call you to order, Mr Simpson.

1. This means that Mrs Wilson replied to someone without asking permission from the chairman/chairwoman.
2. This means Mr Simpson has broken the rules in some way.

Moving to a New Point

Could we move on to item 4 on the agenda?

Now, I'd like to turn to . . .

Can we go on now to . . .

Postponing Discussion

Well, Ladies and Gentlemen, [1]with your approval, I propose to [2]defer this matter until we have more information at our disposal.

If no-one has any objections, I suggest that we leave this matter until our next meeting.

Perhaps we could leave this for [3]the time being. We can come back to it later.

1. ▷ if you agree.
2. ▷ postpone.
3. ▷ now.

Proposing

With the Chair's permission, I [1]move that . . .

[2]Mr Chairman I'll second that [3]motion.

I would like to propose the motion that . . .

Would anyone like to second the motion?

1. Put forward for a vote.
2. After someone has proposed a motion, another person should second the motion before it can be voted on.
3. A carefully worded proposal, to be the subject of the vote.

Moving to a Vote

Perhaps we should take a formal vote on this.

[1]Can I ask for a show of hands?

Let's put it to the vote.

Could we take a vote on it?

Can we move to a vote on this?

1. Participants raise their hands to show their support or opposition.

Voting

In the event of a [1]tie, I would like to remind you that I have the [2]casting vote.

Those for the motion, please?

Those against?

[3]Any abstentions?

The motion [4]is carried [5]unanimously.

The motion has been rejected by 6 votes to 5.

1. Equal numbers of votes for and against the motion.
2. The vote which decides when the votes are equal.
3. If you don't want to vote either for or against, you *abstain*.
4. ▷ has been.
5. Everyone was in favour.

Consensus

It seems that we have a ¹consensus.

Can I take it everyone's in favour?

Are we all agreed on that?

Well, it looks as if we're ²broadly in agreement on this.

1. General agreement.
2. Generally.

Any Other Business

¹Is there any other business?

Any further points?

Is there anything else to discuss?

1. Comes at the end of a meeting; often abbreviated on the agenda to A.O.B.

Closing

I declare the meeting ¹closed. Thank you Ladies and Gentlemen.

That concludes our business for today. Thank you.

Well, I think that ²covers everything.

That's all for today. Thank you.

1. ▷ adjourned until 3 pm, (ie. the meeting will resume at 3).
2. Everything has been discussed.

Mini-Meeting 1

Work in groups of 3 or 4. Take it in turns to be the Chair and hold a meeting.

AGENDA

1. Minutes*
2. Matters Arising
3. Date for Xmas Party
4. The Coffee Machine
5. Any Other Business

* already circulated

Mini-Meeting 2

Work in groups of 3 or 4. Take it in turns to be the Chair and hold a meeting.

AGENDA

1. Minutes
2. Matters Arising
3. Clothing during the summer
     (a) office
     (b) weekly meetings
     (c) outsiders
     (d) A.G.M.
4. A.O.B.

"So far, sergeant, we've narrowed it down to eight suspects."

Getting it all together

Photocopy these two pages and cut up the cards.

Work in groups of 5 or 6. Deal the cards. Ideally each person has the same number of cards.

Check in the book if you have difficulty remembering particular expressions.

When everyone's ready, start the game — the person who has the card saying **BEGIN** starts by introducing whatever topic he/she wants to talk about. Others contribute to the discussion in a way which uses one of their cards. They should place the appropriate card on the table as they say the appropriate expressions. If someone does not use an acceptable expression, the others may challenge him/her and he/she has to take back the card.

The first person to get rid of all his/her cards wins. You can play as often as you want.

BEGIN	**INTRODUCE A NEW POINT**
GIVE AN EXAMPLE	**ASK FOR AN OPINION**
ASK FOR A REACTION	**GIVE AN OPINION**
BRING IN SOMEONE	**SUMMARIZE**
AGREE	**DISAGREE**
INTERRUPT	**TAKE THE FLOOR**

COMMENT	COME BACK TO A POINT
PREVENT AN INTERRUPTION	ASK FOR CONFIRMATION
ASK FOR A REPETITION	CORRECT A MISUNDERSTANDING
REPHRASE	ASK FOR FURTHER INFORMATION
EXPRESS CERTAINTY	MAKE A PROPOSAL
EXPRESS SUPPORT	EXPRESS OPPOSITION
PERSUADE	EXPRESS RESERVATION
REASSURE	EXPRESS UNCERTAINTY
PLAY DOWN A POINT	SAY SOMETHING IS IMPORTANT

1. Most of the time you look at the speaker, but without staring. Sometimes you look elsewhere, for a change and so you do not appear rude.
2. Generally at everybody present, unless you are answering a question asked by a particular person; then you normally look at the person.
3. By the words you use and by sitting back in your chair.
4. Either by raising a finger and waiting or by waiting until there is a suitable pause. This can demand very accurate timing!
5. **Nodding of the head.** This is used in two different ways. It shows acceptance of what has been said. A single nod can also indicate permission to continue speaking. A rapid succession of nods by a listener shows a desire to speak.

Shaking of the head. This is used to express disagreement with what is being said.
Facial expressions. These are difficult to interpret but can give a commentary on what others are saying by showing agreement, disagreement, surprise, disbelief, anger or disappointment. British people feel uncomfortable when others do not use facial expressions.
Eye movements. These play a major role in non-verbal interaction. People look at others to obtain information and feedback. Most people look around more when listening than when speaking. Looking at a speaker also indicates whether you find what the speaker is saying interesting or not.
Gestures with the hands. These can emphasize a point, but are rare In British culture.

Answers

Unit 1

4. Introductory phrases
The following introduce "warnings": Frankly, With respect, To be honest, To put it bluntly.

6. Qualifiers
1. a slight problem 2. some doubts 3. a little more time 4. some production difficulties 5. a slight disagreement 6. some changes 7. I would need a little more time. 8. That would leave me with some slight problems with my Personnel Manager. 9. I really do need a little more time. 10. I think there must be a slight misunderstanding. Of course there are other possibilities — these are only suggestions.

7. Not + very + positive
1. not very convenient 2. not very suitable 3. not a very intelligent/useful suggestion 4. not very good 5. not a very positive 6. not very sensitive 7. not very practical 8. not a very helpful remark 9. not a very constructive approach 10. not a very useful line 11. not very happy.

10. Stressed words
1. Why are you complaining? 2. But I don't really want to. 3. Time to go home! 4. You are taking too long to decide. 5. Please don't delay. 6. Why are you complaining? 7. Not disappointed — annoyed, we feel cheated. 8. This is an important condition. 9. Please give us a decision. *or* We are disappointed/annoyed at the delay. 10. Hurry up!
   There are alternatives, but notice how strong the meaning can be just from **one** extra stress.

Match and Complete, p17
a foregone conclusion, a debatable point, a stop-gap solution, a vested interest, a disastrous step.

Here are the answers to the Match and Complete exercises.

Unit 2

1. run a meeting, weigh the options, close the deal, face the problem, put forward a suggestion.
2. a hasty decision, a preliminary step, a moot point, a short-term solution, overall picture.
3. hammer out a compromise, suffer a setback, miss the point, pose a problem, give an example.
4. in agreement on, on the agenda, on the basis of, on account of, in addition to.
5. on business, in charge of, on behalf of, in certain circumstances, at best, in business.

Unit 3

1. raise the matter, play a role, make an effort, express an opinion, reach a conclusion.
2. a workable solution, a slight misunderstanding, a considered opinion, a fruitful discussion, a dominant factor.
3. answer your question, share your opinion, set your mind at rest, see your point, lend your support.
4. under no circumstances, in concrete terms, in conclusion, in common, in conjunction with.
5. on the contrary, at all costs, in connection with, under consideration, at cross purposes.

Unit 4

1. allocate resources, split hairs, break off negotiations, get results, take steps.
2. various factors, broad agreement, wide-ranging talks, far-reaching repercussions, common knowledge.
3. express our thanks, put our cards on the table, do our best, air our views, keep your options open.
4. a joint venture, a key element, a short adjournment, a reasonable basis, a slight disagreement.
5. in fact, in exchange for, under discussion, in due course, to some extent, into detail.

Unit 5

1. has a word, has the know-how, face the facts, break the deadlock, make a deal.
2. a straightforward matter, a fruitful association, a narrow outlook, ready-made solution, firm commitment.
3. wind up the discussion, deal with the problem, rule out the possibility, make a mistake, overcome the difficulty.
4. in favour of, at my fingertips, at first sight, in general, in this field.
5. on good terms with, in your own interest, under no illusions, to hand, under the impression that.

Unit 6

1. work something out, talk it over, bear what I said in mind, give it our careful consideration, have the facts at my fingertips.
2. a plenary session, a viable alternative, a major contribution, a golden opportunity, a rough guess.
3. hold the meeting, clarify the situation, make a comment, solve the problem, draw the conclusion.
4. in the long run, in the long term, at this juncture, in lieu of, to my knowledge.
5. from the outset, beside the point, at the moment, of note, at this point.

Unit 7

1. jump to conclusions, come to the point, sit on the fence, playing for time, start from scratch.
2. a profitable association, a pressing problem, a short-sighted view, a blunt question, a positive asset.
3. are in the same boat, get down to business, beat about the bush, come to an agreement, go round in circles.
4. in principle, under pressure, at any price, at the present, in practice.
5. out of the question, in all probability, off the record, in some respects, with regard to.

Unit 8

1. reach a decision, broach the subject, chair the meeting, submit a proposal, resolve the difficulty.
2. a frank discussion, a notable exception, a long-term investment, a concrete proposal, a mutual understanding.
3. pose a threat, make a choice, adjourn the meeting, dodge the issue, propose a solution.
4. a heated discussion, a bona fide proposal, a cost-conscious approach, a high priority, a bargaining position.
5. in return for, for the sake of, in this respect, on the safe side, in response to.

Unit 9

1. drive a hard bargain, study a question, reach a stalemate, find a solution, keep an open mind.
2. stumbling block, major disadvantage, an open mind, constructive attitude, a successful outcome.
3. dismiss his offer out of hand, make it clear, leave the problem of finance aside, think it over, take your expenses into account.
4. make any headway, show goodwill, take action, lose face, found some common ground.
5. on schedule, behind schedule, ahead of schedule, at short notice, in the short term.

Unit 10

1. make a concession, call an adjournment, overlook the fact that, pave the way, raise an objection.
2. a positive attitude, a tentative agreement, a feasible project, a last resort, a crucial issue.
3. common ground, grave consequences, protracted negotiations, mutual trust, opening remarks.
4. on the spot, in sight, at stake, at this stage, from the start.
5. for the time being, in view of, on this subject, on the surface, in theory.

Unit 11

1. illustrate the point, undertake a study, have a discussion, clinch the deal, reached a compromise.
2. a serious risk, a fruitful collaboration, a positive outlook, a compromise solution, an on-going programme.
3. offer a compromise, close the meeting, give the floor, tackle the problem, avert a crisis.
4. draw your attention to, meet you halfway, understand your position, put you in the picture, invite your comments on.
5. with a view to, by the way, on the whole, on the verge of, in writing, in a word.